An Artistic Approach to New Testament Literature

❧

Sharon R. Chace

WIPF & STOCK · Eugene, Oregon

AN ARTISTIC APPROACH TO NEW TESTAMENT LITERATURE

Copyright © 2008 Sharon R. Chace. All rights reserved. Except for brief quotations in critical publications or reviews, no part of this book may be reproduced in any manner without prior written permission from the publisher. Write: Permissions, Wipf and Stock, 199 W. 8th Ave., Suite 3, Eugene, OR 97401.

Paperback ISBN 13: 978-1-55635-121-1

Hardcover ISBN 13: 978-1-4982-49096

Dedicated in memory of Doris Brainard,
religious educator and friend.

Contents

※

List of Illustrations / ix
Acknowledgments / xi
Introduction / xiii

1 What Is the New Testament? / 1
2 What Is an Artistic Approach to Biblical Literature? / 4
3 The Synoptic Problem / 8

Part One ※ The Gospel and Growing Proclamation
4 The Gospel according to Mark / 13
5 The Gospel according to Matthew / 22
6 The Gospel according to Luke / 35
7 The Acts of the Apostles / 42

Part Two ※ The Community of the Word
8 The Gospel according to John / 53
9 The Letters of First, Second, and Third John / 68

Part Three ※ Theological Problem and Introduction to Pauline Thought
10 Introducing Paul / 77
11 The First and Second Letters to the Thessalonians / 80
12 The Letter to the Ephesians / 86

Contents

Part Four ❧ The Rest of Paul's Letters
13 The Letter to the Galatians / 97
14 The First Letter to the Corinthians / 101
15 The Second Letter to the Corinthians / 108
16 The Letter to the Romans / 114
17 The Letter to Philemon / 124
18 The Letter to the Philippians / 127

Part Five ❧ Cosmic Christ Served by Good Deeds and Growing Ministry
19 The Letter to the Colossians / 137
20 The Letter of James / 141
21 The First and Second Letters to Timothy, and the Letter to Titus / 149

Part Six ❧ Christians in Crisis
22 The First Letter of Peter / 159
23 The Letter of Jude / 165
24 The Second Letter of Peter / 168

Part Seven ❧ Jesus as Helper, and Christ as Risen Lord
25 The Letter to the Hebrews / 173
26 The Book of Revelation / 181

Bibliography / 195

Illustrations

True Vine, Sharon R. Chace / 65

Jesus's Prayer, Sharon R. Chace / 66

Acknowledgments

THANK YOU to my husband, Ernest. His support and interest help me feel more enthusiastic about my life and work. I am grateful to Fr. Daniel J. Harrington, SJ, for his ongoing, gentle encouragement during and after my days at Weston Jesuit School of Theology. The late Charlotte Currie gave the priceless gift of belief in me, saying "Sharon, you can do anything you want." Thank you to Eleanor Parsons for reading the proofs and to Hope Stafford for her ongoing interest in Christian living. Friend and neighbor Anita Lynn helped me with secretarial details and cups of tea. Finally, I am thankful for the biblical writers and compilers of the book of Proverbs. One verse summarizes how publication of *An Artistic Approach to New Testament Literature* enlivens me: "Hope deferred makes the heart sick, but a desire fulfilled is a tree of life" (13:12).

Introduction

THIS BOOK is for anyone who wants a short guide to the New Testament. My artistic approach is especially appropriate for high school and college students who are interested in the visual arts and want an imaginative supplement to more standard introductions to the New Testament. In a way, I write to my inner self, that eight-year-old girl in a sepia photographic portrait. I wore my best Sunday dress: a candy-striped taffeta blouse with an attached blue skirt. While quiet and dressed in a ladylike fashion for Sunday school, I always spoke my mind, often to the surprise of adults, who did not expect such directness from demure Sharon.

Once, at an evangelical church, I was almost asked to leave Sunday school. My question was upsetting to the Sunday school teachers, who had to caucus to decide how to answer. I asked if the red words in my Bible are really the exact words of Jesus, or are they extra quotation marks? The answer given to me was that they are the exact words of Jesus and they did not want to hear any more doubts. What I should have been told would have gone something like this: *The earthly Jesus was a prophet and preacher but not a writer. His followers, some of them scribes with excellent memories, passed on his sayings by word of mouth and eventually wrote them down. Then the gospel writers collected materials about Jesus as well as his teachings and organized reports, stories, and instructions in their gospels. Sometimes in faithfulness to the person they knew Jesus to be and in the style of other writers in the ancient world, the New Testament authors put a few words into Jesus's mouth that they knew he would or should have said. The writers of the New Testament gospels were more like artists than news reporters. These writers painted pictures of Jesus with words and artistically presented Jesus's parables and stories. Other New Testament writers contributed artfully composed letters, sermons, and theological essays.*

My focus on artistry developed over time. In 1966 I graduated from Albion College in Albion, Michigan, with an art major and English and religion minors. In 1998 I received a Master of Theological Studies (MTS) degree with a biblical concentration, from Weston Jesuit School of Theology in Cambridge, Massachusetts. During my college days, professors of biblical studies focused on historical criticism or examination of the time and

Introduction

place of writing, as well as on meanings in the original life situations of biblical people. They were also interested in source criticism, which is the study of the biblical writers' sources of information and styles of writing. In art history and studio art courses, professors most often emphasized the formal art elements of line, form, color, and texture, whether the students preferred realism or abstract expressionism. In a personal fullness of time, I applied those formal elements to biblical literature.

By the time I entered graduate school, people in many scholarly fields looked at the Bible through their disciplines. Evolving approaches to biblical studies include the psychology of biblical studies, the sociology of biblical studies, and various feminist critiques. As an artist, I approach the Bible artistically. In short, I use artistic characteristics to describe biblical texts and will more fully explain an artistic approach in the second chapter, *What is an Artistic Approach to the New Testament?*

1

What Is the New Testament?

The New Testament is a collection of books with many different kinds of writing, and a record of life in God opening up for the world. The Bible includes the Old Testament, which is the history of the Hebrew or Jewish people's faith and life in God. The Hebrews already had a relationship with God. The New Testament tells the story of how Jesus made this relationship with God possible for all people. In our culture the word *new* often implies "better or improved." However, in the Bible the word *new* often means renewed or updated. Thus, the New Testament is the record of renewed faith and covenant that was updated to include people of all nations. The New Testament records Jesus's life, death, and crucifixion, and (in Christian belief) his resurrection, as well as the spread and development of early Christianity.

There are twenty-seven books in the New Testament. Both Roman Catholics and Protestants agree that these books should be in the New Testament. This official list of books is called the *canon*. The canon, or list of official books, was not decided upon quickly. As early as the end of the second century, Paul's letters and some selections from the gospels were the approved resources for the organization of ritual and social and personal morality of developing Christianity. By the end of the fourth century AD, the list was official. The books that were chosen to be in the canon, or list of sacred books, were helpful to community, in agreement with the basic doctrines of the early church, and associated in some way with the apostles. In summary, the criteria were usefulness and helpfulness. The concept of inspired writings came after approval.

Roman Catholics include more books in the Old Testament canon than do Protestants. The number of books in the Old Testament canon is not an important difference, but it can be confusing. The extra books are the books of the Apocrypha (many Protestant Bibles include these books in a separate section). The Apocrypha can help us understand Judaism and its effects on early Christianity.

Besides the meaning of *canon* as "a list of sacred books," the word canon can mean "rule of life." The Greek word for *canon* means "reed" or "measuring stick," like a ruler. The Bible can be a ruler by which we measure our lives.

Most of us have favorite parts of the Bible. This tendency is sometimes called having "a canon within the canon." Having favorite passages in a favorite book is only natural. Sometimes other passages that have a different emphasis or even a different main idea affect our understanding of our favored verses. Throughout this book, I sometimes refer to counterbalancing passages of Scripture.

The books of the New Testament were not written quickly. During the first third of the first century AD, Jesus lived and preached. During the second third of the first century, people spread his teaching by word of mouth. Repeating Jesus's sayings and stories at homes or in places of worship is called *oral tradition*. Paul wrote between AD 51 and 58. During the last third of the first century, gospel writers wrote down the stories that were told and compiled them. The gospel writers had different ways of organizing their materials about Jesus. Each gospel author adds to our composite picture of Jesus.

Imagine three friends dividing a piece of red licorice into three not-quite-equal pieces to show the stages in which the New Testament came into being. The first piece represents Jesus's teachings. The second, somewhat shorter piece stands for the twenty years when the first preachers shared the good news of God's love in Jesus. The third piece reminds us of the years when writers thought about Jesus and then wrote down all they had heard about Jesus and his way.

There are many kinds of writing in the New Testament. There are short sayings of Jesus and long letters from the Apostle Paul to churches. There are poems and prayers, letters and lists of ancestors. Stories of Jesus's birth and accounts of his passion and last days on earth are part of the New Testament witness. Parables are a very special kind of New Testament story. Parables compare an ordinary activity, like baking bread, to God's reign, or they compare something in nature, such as a vine, to Jesus.

If your family needs to buy groceries, someone makes a grocery list. If you want to talk to God in writing, you might write a prayer or a poem. If you have an interesting tale to tell, you could write a story. If a teacher asks you to write an essay about a person who is running for office, you might listen to the candidate's speech and write a report. If you ran for a leadership position you would state your credentials and tell people why you would be best for the job. If you want your school to sponsor a new club or sport, chances are you will write a speech presenting your most persuasive ideas. You might create slogans or catchy sayings. There are various forms of writing for different purposes in today's world. In biblical times there were also different kinds of writing to convey stories, ideas, history, religious insight and conviction. In the ancient world, rules for reporting were different than the guidelines for today. Still the basic idea holds true that you choose the form of writing that best suits your purpose.

Many writers and editors shared their artistic and literary gifts to give us the story of Jesus and tell us how the Christian faith spread throughout the ancient world.

The World in Front of the Text

Think about the many kinds of biblical writing, including short sayings, letters, prayers, hymns, parables, birth and passion stories, household codes, and sermons. Take a piece of computer or construction paper to represent the Bible as a whole. Then cut or tear pieces of paper in a contrasting color or colors to represent the different kinds of writing in the Bible. Write the names of the kind of writing on the cut or torn paper. Paste the pieces onto the sheet that represents the whole Bible.

A woman who took an experimental version of this course cut her small pieces of paper into shapes that suggested the type of writing. A wavy shape represented hymns. A short piece represented short sayings. An oval, womb shape represented nativity stories. You may use symbolic shapes if you wish.

2

What Is an Artistic Approach to Biblical Literature?

An artistic approach to biblical literature has two main characteristics:

1. Examination of each book of the New Testament from three vantage points: A. The Background; B. The Middle Ground or Text; and C. The Foreground.
2. Description of the text through the formal art elements and other artistic characteristics.

1. Examination of Each Book of the New Testament from Three Vantage Points

A. The background of the text is the historical background and consideration of the basic questions: What? Who? When? Where? Why? What kind of literature is the text being considered? Who wrote it? When was it written? Where was it written? Why was it written?

B. The middle ground, or text, is the biblical text itself in translation from the New Testament Greek. Study of sacred texts is done in tension between the background and the foreground, that is or the world in front of the text that includes our contemporary situation.

C. The foreground is the world in front of the text. In addition to encompassing the writings and artwork of biblical scholars and artists since the New Testament was canonized or became official, the foreground includes your world and what the biblical text means to you.

2. Description of the Text through the Formal Art Elements

An artistic approach is a way of exploring biblical literature by paying attention to the formal art elements that painterly artists designate as *line, form, color* and *texture*. As an artist of both paint and pen, I used these painterly terms to describe verbal texts.

The Use of Line in the Text

Line can mean the plot of a Bible story or a line of thought. For example, parables have a story line. The book of Romans has a very linear argument that Paul makes point by point, line by line. First John contains a circular line of thought that returns to different ways of saying that God is love. Acts is a travel story with a plot line.

Forms of Writing in the Text

Form is the type of writing such as birth story, letter, poem or prayer. Hymns are also part of New Testament literature. Sayings and sermons, genealogical lists, and greetings are types of writing throughout the New Testament.

Use of Color in the Text

Color may be an actual color, such as green or sapphire, mentioned in a biblical passage. I will note the importance of the color green in the chapter on Mark. However, most often color refers to a writer's favorite words or phrases that color a text. For example, Mark likes the word, *immediately*. This word colors his fast-paced writing. Themes or main ideas also color the text, such as the theme of the cross that is especially important in Mark. Faith is a recurring theme in Paul's letters.

Texture in the Text

Texture is the piling up of biblical passages that are related. Sometimes a New Testament verse is a quotation from or allusion to Old Testament passages. The combination of passages gives rich texture and nuances of meanings. Sometimes texture has bridge-building potential between Old and New Testaments and between Judaism and Christianity. My favorite example of an Old Testament passage that is quoted in the New Testament is Habakkuk 2:4: "Look at the proud! Their spirit is not right in them, but the righteous live by their faith." Listen to the Apostle Paul, perhaps in his own rendering of Habakkuk, in Romans 1:17: "For in it the righteousness of God is revealed through faith for faith; as it is written, 'The one who is righteous will live by faith.'" The author of Hebrews develops the meanings of *faith* in chapter 11, often called "the faith chapter." The writer suggested the life-giving context of faith in chapter 10: "but my righteous one will live by faith" (Heb 10:38).

The New Testament is rich in texture. The easiest way to discover texture is to use a study Bible such as *The HarperCollins Study Bible* or *The Oxford Annotated Bible*, which have notes that cite other related biblical passages.

Other Artistic Characteristics

Words that artists use to discuss their paintings can also apply to biblical literature. Such characteristics include "perspective," "focal point," "counterbalance," and "contrast." For example, Mark gives us his perspective on suffering. Christian love is the focal point of First Corinthians. The Gospel of John features contrasting power of darkness and light. Romans and James have counterbalancing thoughts.

Activity: The Foreground

The world in front of the text includes out present time. In the activity suggested in the previous chapter, readers identified various forms of writing in the New Testament. The following activity will help you experience several forms of New Testament literature. You are encouraged to read the following passages:

- Sayings: The beatitudes are sayings of Jesus. You may wish to read them in Matthew 5:1–11.

- Story: One of the most famous stories in the New Testament is the story of the Good Samaritan. You can find it in Luke 10:25–37.

- Parable: To loosely paraphrase C. H. Dodd's classic definition of a parable, a parable is a story that comes from nature, captures our attention, and makes us think. Sheep are part of nature. Sheep often are lost. In the parable of the lost sheep, Matthew can get people's attention by comparing people to lost sheep, and God to the shepherd. You can find this parable in Matthew 18:10–14 and Luke 15:3–7.

- Prayer: The best-known prayer in the New Testament is the *Lord's Prayer*. Matthew and Luke have different versions of Jesus's example of how to pray. You may wish to compare these two variations, in Matthew 6:9–13 and Luke 11:2–4.

- Letter: Paul wrote letters to Christians in the first churches, or Christian assemblies. The letter known as Romans is the letter that is the most discussed by biblical theologians. Chapter 8 is especially important.

- List: If your parents want to study genealogy they will likely make a list of your ancestors. Similarly both Matthew and Luke include a list of Jesus's ancestors in their gospels. Matthew 1:1–17 and Luke 3:23–38.

- Hymn: Philippians 2:6–11 is a hymn about Christ that Paul probably quoted from an earlier writer.

- Homily: Often Hebrews is considered to be a long, philosophical homily or extended sermon.

If you like to write, do you write letters, prayers, reflections, stories, songs, poetic sayings, or lists of your ancestors? You may have literary and artistic connections with biblical writers.

3

The Synoptic Problem

The "Synoptic Problem" is our trying to understand how the Synoptic Gospels relate to one another.[1] By contrasting and comparing the stories and arrangement of sayings in the gospels, readers can spot differences and similarities, which may be confusing. The four gospels in canonical order, which is their order in the Bible, are Matthew, Mark, Luke, and John. The word *gospel* means "good news." At first "good news" meant the theological message of what God had done in Jesus, but later the word *gospel* came to mean a literary form that narrates and proclaims. Matthew, Mark, and Luke are called the "Synoptic Gospels" because they tell the story of Jesus in generally the same way. They have a common understanding of Jesus as Son of Man, Son of David, Son of God, and Messiah. These gospels present a common outline of Jesus's gathering of disciples, ministry of teaching and healing, journey to Jerusalem, passion and death. The word *synoptic* comes from a New Testament Greek word that means "seeing the whole together."[2] Despite presenting the same essential outline of Jesus's life, the Synoptic Gospels have distinctive characteristics. For example, Mark wrote to Gentile Christians and emphasized Jesus as the suffering Son of Man. Luke also writing to Gentile Christians, presented Jesus as prophet. Writing to Jewish Christians, Matthew stressed Jesus as fulfillment of Scripture.[3]

The Gospel of John is very different in style, content, and, to some extent, cultural context from the Synoptic Gospels.[4] John presents a three-year ministry of Jesus in contrast to the sense of a one-year ministry in Matthew, Mark, and Luke. Jesus goes to Jerusalem more often in the Gospel of John than he does in the other gospels. While the kingdom of God is a primary focus of the Synoptic Gospels, the Gospel of John

---

1. Harrington, *How to Read the Gospels*, 22.
2. Duling and Perrin, *New Testament*, 605.
3. Harrington, *How to Read the Gospels*, 23.
4. Ibid., *Who is Jesus?* 60–61.

pictures Jesus as revealer.[5] Because of their beliefs about Jesus, people in John's community had been asked to leave their former synagogue. As you can imagine, hurt feelings must have affected the social context and how John's people felt about the world.

The prevailing answer[6] to the Synoptic Problem is called the Two-Source Theory. This solution claims that Matthew and Luke used two written sources to compile their gospels. These two written sources are the Gospel of Mark and the Q source. Mark, the first written gospel, was written in about 70 AD. This gospel is the primary source for the story line of Jesus's life and ministry in Matthew and Luke. The designation of the letter *Q* for the second source for Matthew and Luke probably is derived from the German word *Quelle*, which means "source."[7] This Q source is found in Matthew and Luke but is mainly missing in Mark. This Q source is composed mostly of Jesus's sayings, written in Greek. An estimated date for the Q source is 50–70 AD.[8] In addition to Mark and Q, the writers of Matthew and Luke had their own sources. Luke's source that Matthew did not have is called *Special L*. Matthew's source that Luke did not share is called *Special M*. The wise men in Matthew come from Matthew's source, and the shepherds in Luke are from Luke's source. Luke's special materials, combined with his literary skill, shape the short stories of the Good Samaritan and the Prodigal Son. Attention to the sources that the gospel writers used helps readers appreciate the writing process.

---

5. Ibid., *How to Read the Gospels*, 38–39.
6. Duling and Perrin, *New Testament*, 605.
7. Ibid., *New Testament*, 603–4.
8. Ibid., *The New Testament*,107, 603–4.

Part One

The Gospel and Growing Proclamation

4

The Gospel according to Mark
Take Up Your Cross

Background

MATTHEW IS the first book in the New Testament, so why does this book begin with Mark? Mark was the first person to write a New Testament gospel, which seems to be a form of writing that he invented.[1] Therefore Mark is the earliest gospel.

Who Was Mark?

According to Papias, an early church bishop of Asia Minor, Mark may have been an interpreter of Peter. (I heard the Papias story in college, and it has come around to favor again.) Mark heard stories about Jesus and probably read some. He spoke Greek but struggled to write it well. The most emotional of the evangelists, Mark saw the world through dark glasses. He talks about the disciples as having no faith (4:40) and wonders if they will ever understand his mission and forthcoming suffering (8:21). In a word, in Mark they are "uncomprehending."[2]

Mark was very focused on the meaning of the cross and suffering. Mark's belief (recorded in 10:45) that "the Son of Man came not to be served, but to serve, and to give his life as a ransom for many," is like a hearty filling of a sandwich. The two slices of sandwich bread are two stories of restored sight in 8:22–26 and 10:46–52. My sandwich analogy is a take-off on scholarly commentary. "Very important for the structure of the gospel as a whole is something like a large 'sandwich' in the middle of the gospel (8:22—10:52)."[3] In summary, Duling and Perrin go on to

---

1. Harrington, *Who is Jesus?* 21.
2. Ibid., *How to Read the Gospels*, 23.
3. Duling and Perrin, *New Testament*, 304–5.

say that the section in which Jesus tried to explain the necessity for his suffering and gives three passion predictions (8:27—10:45) sandwiched between two stories of people being given their sight. The passion predictions are in 8:31, 9:31 and 10:33–34. The stories about restored sight are in 8:22–26 and 10:46–52.

What Did Mark Write?

Mark wrote a gospel. In addition to describing a form of writing, the word *gospel* also means proclamation about God's love shown in the life, death, and (in Christian belief) resurrection of Jesus.

Mark's gospel is something like biographies of famous leaders in the Greek world who were willing to die for their people, as Jesus did. More important, Mark's gospel is a theological story about Jesus the Christ. While Mark did not use the best Greek, he did the best he could to preserve stories about Jesus's life, teachings, and passion and therefore used his abilities to the glory of God.

To Whom Did Mark Write?

He wrote to Christians who were persecuted. These Gentile Christians (that is, Christians who had not been Jews first) needed to know more about Jewish customs. Mark's audience was an early sect that expected that Christ would return shortly.

The picture of Jesus that Mark painted with words spoke to Mark's community. Mark's Jesus is the suffering son of God and Son of Man, who will in the future bring in the kingdom in all its fullness. Mark was not aware that in time Christians would understand Jesus as the second person of the Trinity. Yet to Mark, the Son of Man is more than is a prophet. Jesus is akin, perhaps even in his own mind, to a high-ranking saint, who fulfills the role of Son of Man who is similar to the "One like a human being coming with the clouds of heaven" in Daniel 7:13. Biblical scholar Morna D. Hooker says that in Mark's gospel Jesus accepted the calling of the saints of the Most High, who suffer at the hands of God's enemies who are promised final vindication.[4]

When and Where Did Mark Write His Gospel?

The Gospel of Mark was written in about 70 AD, likely in Rome.

---

4. Hooker, *Gospel according to Saint Mark*, 90.

The Text

Color

Mark's favorite words that color his writing are *no faith*, *amazed* or *astonished*, and *immediately*. He often describes the disciples as not having faith. Jesus's deeds amaze people. Characters take immediate action. Likewise, Mark's story moves quickly. In order to make transitions in his stories, he often wrote, "Truly I tell you."

In the story of the feeding the five thousand (6:30–44), Marks tells us that the people sat down in groups on the green grass. He is the only evangelist to tell us the color of the grass in feeding stories. (John does tell us there was a lot of grass in the place.) His mentioning the color green suggests that Mark might have been thinking of Psalm 23 and understood Jesus as the Good Shepherd. Or maybe, emotional Mark was just more sensitive to color than Matthew, Luke, and John.

Texture

The very first verse in Mark is a textured allusion to Isaiah 40:9 and 52:7 and 61:1, where "good news" suggests glad tidings of salvation. Nuances of meaning are heralding and announcing, which is what John the Baptist did for Jesus.

Line

The plot line is summarized in the parable of the wicked tenants (Mark 12:1–12). Jesus the Christ, as beloved Son of God in keeping with God's will, but with the help of some Jewish leaders, had to suffer. Mark's line can be broken into two parts:

1. Chapters 1–8. Jesus teaches, preaches, and heals in Galilee.
2. Chapters 9–16. Jesus takes his disciples on an educational trip between Galilee and Jerusalem and predicts his forthcoming suffering and death. The end of the gospel is like a two-pronged fork because there are two endings, which are a short ending and a long ending. The short ending ends with the empty tomb, while the longer ending rounds out the story with postresurrection appearances.

PART ONE: THE GOSPEL AND GROWING PROCLAMATION

The Story Line
Part 1: Proclamation of God's Reign

Jesus teaches, preaches, and heals in Galilee through powerful words and deeds.

Chapter 1

Instead of starting with a story about Jesus's birth as do Matthew and Luke, Mark fast-forwards to the proclamation of John the Baptist—that someone more powerful than John will come. Jesus is baptized by John and tempted in the wilderness where he dwells peacefully with wild animals. Jesus calls his first disciples; and he heals a distraught man, Simon's mother-in-law, and a leper.

Chapter 2

Jesus tells a paralyzed man that his sins are forgiven before telling him to take up his pallet and walk. Because Jesus's power to forgive sin is a new thing, people are amazed. Explaining that he came not for the righteous but for sinners, Jesus eats with sinners and tax collectors. He states that the Sabbath was made for humanity.

Chapter 3

Jesus backs up his assertion that the Sabbath was made for humanity by healing a man with a withered hand. Jesus appoints the twelve disciples and declares that his family is the people who do God's will.

Chapter 4

Jesus tells parables about the kingdom or reign of God. The parable of the sower (4:3–9) is about Jesus's teachings taking root and growing in good soil. Mark's explanation of the parable is like a sermon for children in the early church. The following stories of the growing seed, which is unique to Mark; and the mustard seed that grows into a shrub large enough to shelter birds suggests the growth of the kingdom from small to large.

Mark captures a vivid picture of Jesus's power over chaos, symbolized by Jesus's power to calm the storm. The disciples panic with fright when a storm blows up and tosses their boat around. In Mark's story of faith, Jesus puts his trust in God and goes to sleep. After Jesus's disciples wake him up, Jesus commands the sea to be still, and the wind and the sea obey.

Chapter 5

Jesus heals a distraught man by driving the man's demons into pigs that rush into the sea and drown. This man had been sick, but he was smart enough to recognize Jesus as *Son of the Most High God*. People are amazed. Jesus heals a woman with a flow of blood and declares that her faith has made her well. Then Jesus heals a twelve-year-old girl thought to be dead, but who was sleeping.

Chapter 6

Jesus teaches in his hometown synagogue where people are astounded yet dismiss Jesus. Rejected in his hometown of Nazareth, Jesus cannot do deeds of power there. Jesus sends out the twelve. John the Baptist is killed after challenging Herod's ethics. Jesus feeds the hungry people, who are like sheep without a shepherd. In this story of the miraculous feeding of five thousand people with five loaves of bread and two fish, the people sit on the green grass.

Jesus walks on water and tells his disciples, who think that he is a ghost, to not be afraid for *It is I*. Mark's implication is that Jesus is to his disciples like God was in Moses's experience. In Exodus 3:13, God reveals God's self to Moses with the words, *I AM WHO I AM*.

Chapter 7

Jesus identifies destructive attitudes and actions. Jesus is not concerned about eating patterns but does care about spiritual food poisoning that includes theft and murder. Instead of being overly tied to food regulations, Jesus redefines ritual purity as righteous or good behavior.

Jesus broadens his ministry to include non-Jews by healing the Syrophoenician woman's daughter. Mark's Gentile audience would not lose the message that they are also in God's care. Jesus then cures a deaf man with a speech impediment. Restored hearing symbolizes the ability to hear religiously. Again people are astonished.

Chapter 8

Mark relates another feeding story. Then, Jesus heals a blind man. This healing takes place in two stages. At first, after Jesus puts saliva in the blind man's eyes, he sees people, but not clearly. The people are like "trees walking." Then after Jesus's second touch, the man sees more clearly, as eventually the disciples will in the rest of the story. Therefore, this story of improving sight sets the stage for the second part of Mark's gospel when Jesus takes his disciples on an educational trip on which Jesus instructs them about his identity and the cost of discipleship.[5] "A journey through Galilee begins with Jesus's second prediction of his passion (9:30–32), which once again the disciples do not understand."[6] Some learning took place on the educational journey. Following the story of the blind man (9:22–26), Peter articulates his insight and faith by saying to Jesus, "You are the Messiah" (9:27–30). Jesus again foretells his death (9:31–33) and calls his followers to take up their cross and follow him, while telling his disciples that those who lose their lives for his sake will find their lives (9:34).

Part 2: Extension of Jesus's Ministry

Jesus takes his disciples on an educational trip between Galilee and Jerusalem and predicts his forthcoming suffering and death.

Chapter 9

The story of the transfiguration symbolizes Jesus's participation in God's glory and may reflect a mystical experience of Jesus's union with God. Jesus heals an epileptic boy through prayer. The boy's father is moved to say, "I believe; help my unbelief!" Again Jesus foretells his death and resurrection. The disciples do not understand and are afraid to ask. Greatness is defined as welcoming children, who symbolize the powerless. There are radical sayings, about not causing other people to stumble in faith, that are strong words in order to make the points. Salt is a powerful metaphor of preservation and self-giving. Jesus instructs his disciples to be salty and at peace with one another.

Chapter 10

Jesus's teachings on divorce show high regard for women. These teachings make it harder for the men of his day to divorce their wives. Jesus blesses little children. Stressing the hazards of wealth, he tells a rich person that it is easier for a camel to pass through the eye of a needle than for a rich person to enter heaven. He counterbalances that thought with the assurance that with God all things are possible. On the road, which is a metaphor for discipleship, Jesus tells of his death for a third time. He heals a blind man named Bartimaeues, saying that the man's faith made him well.

---

5. Harrington, *How to Read the Gospels*, 26.
6. Brown, *Introduction to the New Testament*, 140.

Chapters 11–12

Jesus's entering Jerusalem is a turning point of Mark's gospel. Jesus enters Jerusalem on the day that Christians call Palm Sunday. He cleans the temple and speaks about the power to move mountains. In chapter 12, Jesus addresses the issue of taxes and amazes people with his instructions to give the emperor those things that are his, and to give God the things that belong to God. Jesus addresses questions about the resurrected life. Writing with texture, Mark tells us that Jesus says to an inquiring scribe: that the first commandment is to love God and our neighbor as ourselves. The scribe then realizes the truth in the Old Testament passage, Hosea 6:6. In summary, this passage, which was part Jesus's sacred Scriptures, states that love of neighbor is more important than burnt offerings. Jesus says to the scribe, "You are not far from the kingdom of God" (12:34).

Chapter 13

The kingdom of God will come completely in the fullness of God's own time. This chapter, which is sometimes called "the little apocalypse," stresses the future aspects of the kingdom. No one really knows what the reader is to understand by *desolating sacrilege*. However, in any age when the present is bleak, watchfulness and accountability are dimensions of hopefulness. Mark 13 is a blend of Jesus's sayings and the thoughts of leaders in the first-century church. So this chapter is as much about the people of the first-century church as it is about the future. Discipleship is a major theme, and persecution is predicted. Yet the followers of Jesus could find hope through belief in future vindication.

Chapter 14

Two days before the Passover, a few leaders look for a way to arrest and kill Jesus. An unnamed woman in Bethany anoints Jesus with costly ointment. The disciples criticize her, but Jesus says that she has performed a "good service" (NRSV) or, in another translation, "a beautiful thing" for him (NIV). In the upper room, the disciples join Jesus for the Passover. Jesus tells them that one of them will betray him. They commune in the breaking of bread, and go into the garden of Gethsemane to pray. Jesus prays, asking for whatever God wants. In keeping with the theme of fulfillment of the Scriptures, Judas betrays Rabbi Jesus with a kiss of identification. Peter also denies Jesus and weeps.

Chapter 15

Jesus responds wisely to Pilate. Jesus stands before Pilate answering the question of whether or not he is the King of the Jews with the ambiguous statement: "You say so." He is handed over to be crucified. Quoting from Psalm 22, Jesus on the cross asks, "My God, my God, why have you forsaken me?" Scholars disagree over whether or not readers are to conclude that because the rest of the psalm includes words of confidence in God's vindication that Jesus knew that ultimately he was not forsaken.[7]

In verse 38, the curtain of the temple is torn in two—possibly symbolizing that God's presence is no longer hidden. All people have access to God in a dawning new age. The study notes in the HarperCollins Study Bible state that the words *was torn* perhaps means the temple's eradication and unmediated access to God created by Jesus's death.[8]

In the centerpiece or focal point of the passion story, the centurion confesses that truly this man is God's son. Some women who had followed Jesus do not abandon him. Joseph of Arimathea, a good man and respected member of the council, buries him.

Chapter 16

Three women are there for Jesus and visit the tomb, finding it empty. A young man wearing a white robe explains that Jesus has been raised. Amazement and terror fill the women, who remain silent. The longer ending rounds out Mark's gospel with postresurrection stories that are a collage formed from incidents in the other gospels. This composite closing ends with a call to go into the world and proclaim the good news.

The World in Front of the Text

Jesus experienced rejection, and many other people have also been rejected or have known someone who has not found acceptance. Do you have ideas about how to embrace your own pain from rejection or how to help other people who are outside circles of concern?

If you have access to the book *Medieval Art: Painting–Sculpture–Architecture, 4th–14th Century*, by James Snyder, find a picture of Mark that captures his personality.[9] The picture is *Saint Mark*, which is an illustration in the Gospel Book of Ebbo. Mark looks heavenward at a lion and seems to be in an inspired, emotional trance. Swirling lines in his robe

---

7. *New Interpreter's Bible*, 8:723.
8. *HarperCollins Study Bible*, 1950.
9. Snyder, *Medieval Art: Painting–Sculpture–Architecture, 4th–14th Century*, 217.

and a cascading waterfall in the background suggest spiritual intensity. Mark's fingers rest on an open book as if God wanted him to either write his gospel or find meaningful biblical passages in the Hebrew Scriptures.

5

The Gospel according to Matthew
The Kingdom Is Near

Background
Who Was Matthew?

MATTHEW WAS an anonymous, Greek-speaking author named after the Matthew who had been Jesus's disciple. A verse in his gospel paints a cameo of him as a scribe in training for the kingdom of God, who draws out of his treasure what is new and what is old (13:52). As a scribe, Matthew uses his skills to draw upon old traditions and new ideas. In Matthew's day, scribes were more than notetakers because they had their own thoughts. Being comfortable with the complexities of parables is a characteristic of scribes, as described in the book of Sirach, which is one of the seven books in the Apocrypha. (In Catholic Bibles, these added books, which Roman Catholics consider as part of the canon, are interspersed among the uncontested books of the Old Testament, while in many Protestant Bibles, the apocryphal books are often in an appendix.[1]) The scribe, as described by Sirach, is discerning: "He seeks out the wisdom of all the ancients, and is concerned with prophecies; he preserves the sayings of the famous and penetrates the subtleties of parables; he seeks out the hidden meanings of proverbs and is at home with the obscurities of parables" (Sirach 39:1–3).

Matthew was attracted to Jesus, the wise teacher who spoke in parables, so Matthew recorded and organized Jesus's teachings and stories. My deduction is that because Matthew was pictured as a scribe in training and because he included parables in his gospel, he, like the scribes in Sirach, was comfortable with ambiguity or obscurity of parables. Parables do encourage thought about their meanings.

---

1. Harrington, *Invitation to the Apocrypha*, 4.

When and Where Did Matthew Write?

Matthew wrote between 85 and 90 AD, when the church started to take shape. The main argument for Palestine as the place of composition is Matthew's record of opposing movements of the scribes and Pharisees, who lived in Palestine.

Matthew's gospel resembles Greek biographies about individual heroes. Yet Matthew cares about community and *Christology*, a word that means "teachings about Christ." His gospel is a basic document for a new community of Jews and Gentiles joined together as a worshipping body in the spirit of Christ. Matthew's community seems to have been relatively wealthy.[2] His church has moved away from the synagogue.[3] Matthew's community was in conflict with outsiders and facing some internal disarray, such as the threat of false prophets (7:15–20) and some inclination to not follow the Torah (5:17–20).[4]

Matthew paints a picture of a wise and loving God who established Sabbath rest from the beginning of creation. He bases his story on Mark's outline. However, Matthew has his own sources, including the *Special M* material, and a sayings source that scholars call *Q*, which Luke also uses. Matthew uses his sources in his masterpiece—the collection of Jesus's teachings called the Sermon on the Mount. Matthew presents Jesus's additional teachings in blocks of sermons.

Matthew paints a picture of Jesus as the Son of God, Son of David, and royal Messiah. He sees Jesus as the fulfillment of the law, a kind of new or updated Moses. Matthew's Jesus offers both challenge and comfort.

Why Did Matthew Write?

Matthew was motivated by a religious crisis that faced all Jews in the late first century.[5] The temple had been destroyed. Judaism was in transition. The main question was, how could Judaism continue without the temple? So Matthew explains Jesus as the promise to Israel and fulfillment of Hebrew law. Moses taught his people on Mount Sinai. Matthew's Jesus preaches on a mountain. The clear connotation is that Jesus is a Moses figure. For Matthew, Jesus is the founder of the true Israel and the new

---

2. *New Interpreter's Bible*, 8:104.
3. Fuller, "Matthew," 951.
4. Duling and Perrin, *New Testament*, 335.
5. Harrington, *Who is Jesus?* 29.

interpreter of the law. Thus, in Matthew's thought, people gathered around Jesus could carry on the most authentic or best form of Judaism.[6]

Matthew also wants to explain the importance of Peter in the developing Christian movement. In Matthew's tradition, Peter was seen as a representative figure.[7] In answer to Jesus's question about himself, Peter answered saying, "You are the Messiah" (16:16). Jesus said, "And I tell you, you are Peter, and on this rock I will build my church, and the gates of Hades will not prevail against it" (16:18). Protestants and Catholics have disagreed about the meanings of this passage often according to the prevailing views in their respective churches:

> One of the achievements of contemporary ecumenical scholarship, however, is that both Protestant and Roman Catholic scholars generally agree that the original meaning of the text is that Jesus builds the church on Peter as the foundation (contrary to previous Protestant views) rather than on Peter's confession or Peter's faith, and that the position Peter held was unique and unrepeatable (contrary to previous Roman Catholic views).[8]

In my opinion, both Peter's confession of faith in Jesus and his leadership of an early Christian community as assigned by Jesus helped the church to have a strong start.

Sometimes Matthew uses biting language. Strong words can be the language of separation. As a teenager may say hurtful things to parents while growing into her- or himself, the young church, or Jewish Christian sect, had to do battle with older religious groups with different ideas about how to live religiously without the temple.

Artistic Features of the Text

Segmented Line

As an artistic writer, Matthew understands history as a segmented line. The genealogy or list of Jesus's ancestors is the first segment. The second section on the line is Jesus's time on earth, when faithful people worshipped. The third segment is the fulfillment of the kingdom.

---

6. Harrington, *Who Is Jesus?* 29–30.
7. *New Interpreter's Bible*, 8:103.
8. Ibid., 8:347.

Catchwords That Capture Form

Catchwords that capture Matthew's shaping of his gospel are *building blocks* and *bookends*. The sermons are building blocks that summarize the teachings of Jesus. Calling Jesus *Emmanuel*, which means "God is with us," in the beginning of Matthew, and stating at the end of the book that Jesus will be present with his followers are statements that create thematic bookends that promise God's presence.

Color Words

Like Mark, Matthew also has favorite words that color his text by highlighting his points. In contrast to the disciples in Mark, who sometimes had "no faith," Matthew often describes the disciples as having "little faith" (6:30; 8:26; 14:31; 16:8). Matthew also likes the words, *perfect* (5:48: 19:21), and *fruit* (3:08; 3:10; 7:17: 12:33). *Perfect* is a word that sometimes frightens people. In Matthew, *perfect* connotes "wholeness."[9] Throughout the Bible, fruit is a symbol of righteousness. Matthew's most favorite word is *fulfill*. This word implies "to complete or to make whole." Matthew constantly uses it to show that Jesus fulfilled the words of the prophets. These fulfillment citations based on Old Testament passages are richly textured.

Headlines and Highlights of the Text

Genealogy

Matthew begins with a list of Jesus's ancestors: "An account of the genealogy of Jesus the Messiah, the son of David, the son of Abraham"(1:1). The amazing thing about this list is the inclusion of women. Ruth was from Moab. Rahab was a righteous Gentile who helped the Israelites. When I was in college, the professor stressed that the inclusion of Ruth, a Moabite, suggests a note of universality in Jesus's family tree. In graduate school in the 1990s, the spin was that the inclusion of women in the genealogy means that women as well as men can be models of faithfulness. The combined hints are that the kingdom will be inclusive.

---

9. Harrington, *The Gospel of Matthew*, 90; see also Brown, "Meaning of Perfection," 24–29.

Birth Story Foreshadows Wisdom Theme

Chapters 1 and 2 contain a birth story of Jesus. This story includes wise men who follow the star to Bethlehem. Jesus, who is born in the city of David, will be the Son of David and more. He also will grow up to be the Wise Teacher. When the star stops, the wise men are overwhelmed with joy (for shepherds, see Luke's account). Before Jesus is born, an angel tells Joseph in a dream that Mary will have a son to be named *Jesus*. The angel's words are in a little poem that says the people will also call Jesus, "Emmanuel." "All this took place to fulfill what had been spoken through the prophet; 'Look, the virgin shall conceive and bear a son, and they shall name him Emmanuel' which means, God is with us" (1:22–23).

Because Jesus is wise like the wise men, his birth narrative foreshadows the grown-up Jesus. People in Jesus's hometown are astounded, and ask where Jesus got his wisdom (13:54). Jesus, in Matthew's account, is a spokesperson for God and personifies wisdom. He is identified with personified wisdom yet without a doctrine of preexistence.[10] "Matt 11:27 presents Jesus as divine wisdom incarnate. Those who know him know the Father—which is after all the ultimate in wisdom."[11] Another example of Jesus's wisdom is his concern for Sabbath rest (11:25–30), a theme that occurs throughout the Bible and has universal implications.

Chapter 2 also tells us that an angel of the Lord appeared to Joseph in another dream and told him to take Mary and Jesus to Egypt to get away from Herod and his evil plans. Another dream tells Joseph when it is time to move his family to Galilee. Towards the end of the gospel, Pilate's wife will learn in a dream that Jesus was a just man. Dreams were a source of wisdom and guidance.

Baptism and Temptation

In chapter 3, John the Baptist appears on the scene proclaiming repentance and that the kingdom of God is near. He baptizes people with water but says that the one coming after him will baptize with the Holy Spirit. He honors Jesus's request for baptism. When Jesus is baptized, a voice from heaven says, "This is my Son, the Beloved, with whom I am well pleased" (v. 17).

In chapter 4, Matthew tells the story of Jesus's experience in the wilderness. Jesus resists all temptations to worldly power and fame. The kingdom of God would not be about earthly power and fame but rather about

---

10. *New Interpreter's Bible*, 8:356.
11. Harrington, *Gospel of Matthew*, 170.

God's transcendent reign and peace. To use categories of today, Matthew was more interested in the political dimensions of Jesus's temptations, whereas it seems to me Mark has ecological implications and suggests, in the spirit of Genesis, that creation and the animal kingdom are good.

Sensitive Mark may have picked up on Jesus's way with animals and, implying more than he knew, anticipated something of what we call ecological concerns today. Of course these thoughts are conjecture. The notes in the *HarperCollins Study Bible* say that the significance of Jesus's being with the wild beasts is unclear; it may suggest the restoration of paradisaical conditions.[12] Because Mark struggled with language, my sense is that he might have thought conclusions, but stopped sort of clearly stating them. It would be my hope that Mark would want his readers to use their imaginations and fill in the gaps. Mark did say, "And the Spirit immediately drove him into the wilderness. He was in the wilderness forty days, tempted by Satan; and he was with the wild beasts; and the angels waited on him" (1:12–13). It seems to me that the friendly wild beasts in Mark that did not eat one another (or Jesus) suggest that Mark's Jesus was a bit like St. Francis of Assisi, who cared for animals. And for years, this passage has reminded me of Edward Hicks's paintings with a peaceable kingdom theme based on Isaiah 11:6–9. Preachers and artists, writers and theologians, can suggest how people can care for animals and the environment in ways that make for peace.

Matthew the scribe tells a longer story about the temptation of Jesus than Mark does (4:1–11). In summary, Jesus is led by the Spirit into the wilderness to be tempted by the devil. This tempter tells Jesus that if Jesus was the Son of God to turn stones into bread. Jesus refuses saying, "It is written, 'One does not live by bread alone, but by every word that comes from the mouth of God'" (v. 4). Jesus also refused to throw himself down from the pinnacle of the temple to prove that he is the Son of God saying that it was written, "Do not put the Lord your God to the test" (v. 7). Finally, the devil promises Jesus all the kingdoms of the world if Jesus would worship him. Rejecting the promise of earthly kingship, Jesus insists on worship of God and service to God. Matthew's picture suggests that Jesus knew that quest for political power can become idolatrous. The secular as well as religious import for today could be that unchecked political ambitions are ruinous.

The temptation story in Matthew has for years been part of Sunday school lore that Jesus withstood temptation to live only for earthly pleasures, to do magic, or to be an earthly ruler. The first memory I have of

---

12. *HarperCollins Study Bible*, 1918.

that general thrust is an eighth-grade Sunday school class in a Universalist Church (c.1957) taught by the director of religious education, the late Nancy Hildonen, who was a United Church of Christ minister. I would like to think that Matthew the scribe who was comfortable with ambiguity of parables would be happy that people over the centuries have thought about his writings, their many possible meanings, and how to actualize them.

Sermons as Building Blocks

Chapters 5–7: First Sermon, *The Sermon on the Mount*

The best-known sermon in Matthew is "the Sermon on the Mount," which is a collection of Jesus's teachings. This sermon shows how Jesus fulfills the Law and the Prophets. Acts of piety, undivided hearts, showing mercy, and bearing spiritual fruit are characteristics of righteous living in this well-loved passage.

Chapter 5 includes the beatitudes. These are spiritual blessings that will come to people in God's time. In anyone's present, these sayings give comfort because each unhappy spiritual condition has a compensating solace. The eighth beatitude (5:10) is redactional—that is to say, with an editor's added information about Matthew's church. In the past, the synagogue persecuted the people that it addresses because they adhered to the Messianic Torah of Jesus rather than the Mosaic Torah. The final Beatitude (v. 11) envisages the possibility of present persecution by the Roman outsiders in the time of Domitian (81–96 AD).[13]

In the rest of the sermon, Matthew proclaims Jesus's instructions to be the salt of the earth and challenges people, then and now, to let our light shine to the glory of God:

> You are the salt of the earth; but if salt has lost its taste, how can it's saltiness be restored? It is no longer good for anything, but is thrown out and trampled underfoot. You are the light of the world. A city built on a hill cannot be hid. No one after lighting a lamp puts it under the bushel basket, but on the lampstand, and it gives light to all in the house. In the same way, let your light shine before others, so that they may see your good works and give glory to your Father in heaven. (vv. 13–16)

The metaphor of salt adds a little local color of Palestine. Salt from the Dead Sea, which is mixed with gypsum, tastes stale. Being like salt that flavors with goodness is a good way to live.

---

13. Fuller, "Matthew," 956.

Jesus tells his followers that he has come not to destroy the law but to fulfill it. The Torah remains in force. Yet Matthew clearly believes that the Jesus program—or the way of making the Torah real or actualizing it—is superior to the more narrow interpretation of the scribes and Pharisees. Often Christians use the term *legalistic*, but *narrow* is a description that is fairer. Jesus called his listeners—and Matthew instructed his readers—to pray for enemies. Praying for our enemies is a very grown-up, mature, whole, or complete spirituality.

Without denying the importance of public worship, Matthew chapter 6 starts with affirmation of private prayer in contrast to showy, public displays of private prayer. Forms of Jewish piety, including almsgiving, prayer, and fasting are independent of the temple and can be practiced anywhere. Matthew passes on Jesus's model of prayer, known today as the Lord's Prayer (6:9–13). This prayer asks that God's will be done on earth as it is in heaven, and thus gives a glimpse of God's kingdom as a place where all people acknowledge the holiness of God. Jesus observes the natural world and draws lessons from it: "Consider the lilies of the field, how they grow; they neither toil nor spin, yet I tell you, even Solomon in all his glory was not clothed like one of these" (6:28–29). The call to strive first for the kingdom of God offers perspective.

In chapter 7, Jesus warns about seeing a speck in a neighbor's eye without seeing the log in our own eye. Matthew affirms Jesus's conviction that our Father in heaven gives good things to people who ask. This chapter concludes with the golden rule: "In everything do to others as you would have them do to you; for this is the law and the prophets" (v. 12). Thus, Jesus summarizes and simplifies the law. In Matthew, the authority of the Torah is in Christ. Righteousness, as Matthew understands it, is conduct based on Jesus's interpretation of the law. Matthew 7 concludes with a parable of a wise man who built his house upon a rock. People who act upon Jesus's words will be like that man who used solid rock for his foundation.

Chapters 8–10: First Intervening Block

A story between the first and second sermons shows Matthew's concern for the developing church (8:23–27). In Matthew's account of the stilling of the storm, Matthew shifts from Mark's emphasis on a natural miracle that shows Jesus's power to an allegory of following Jesus. The little boat may even symbolize the church. The thrust is trust in both the power of Jesus and the future of the Christian movement.

Chapters 10—11:1: Second Sermon, *The Missionary Discourse*

This second sermon, which is addressed to the disciples, is sometimes called the "missionary discourse." Jesus summons the twelve apostles: Simon Peter, Andrew, James, John, Philip, Bartholomew, Thomas, Matthew, another James, Thaddaeus, Simon, and Judas Iscariot (who would betray him). Jesus sends out the twelve with the authority to cure the lost sheep of Israel: "The kingdom has come near. Cure the sick, raise the dead, cleanse the lepers, cast out demons'" (10:7–8). "If anyone will not welcome you or listen to our words, shake off the dust from your feet as you leave that house or town" (10:14). Speaking of persecutions to come, Matthew quotes Jesus. Telling his disciples that he is sending them out "like sheep into the midst of wolves," Jesus instructs his disciples to be as wise as serpents and as gentle as doves (10:16). Matthew's Jesus promises help: "When they hand you over, do not worry about how you are to speak or what you are to say; for what you are to say will be given to you at that time" (10:19). Have no fear, says Jesus. "Do not fear those who will kill the body but not the soul. Are not two sparrows sold for a penny? Yet not one of them will fall to the ground apart from your Father. And even the hairs of your head are counted. So do not be afraid; you are of more value than many sparrows" (10:29–31).

The cost of discipleship will be family division but also the finding of one's own best life. Sometimes people in Matthew's community had to choose between family and faith. The three major monotheistic religions—Islam, Judaism, and Christianity—have the potential of becoming violent in the name of God. It is important to consider context. In verse 34 of chapter 10, Jesus says (in my paraphrase), do not think I have come to bring peace but a sword. This poetic metaphor of the sword suggests that sometimes it is necessary to cut family ties as a result of faith. The poetry makes it clear that Jesus was not talking literally but proverbially, as in the style of the scribes. Hospitality symbolized by giving a cup of cold water in Jesus's name will be rewarded.

Chapters 11–12: Second Intervening Block

Starting in chapter 11, verse 2, Matthew draws upon Mark and Q. Jesus is Wisdom's spokesperson in 12:28–30. Comforting his disciples, Jesus promises to give rest and says, "For my yoke is easy, and my burden is light" (11:28). Different biblical images sometimes give counterbalance. The easy yoke as rabbinical metaphor for joyous obedience to the Torah is counterpoint to the point of the cost of discipleship. Chapter 12 reminds us that God desires mercy and not sacrifice. Jesus is pictured as God's servant, in whose name the Gentiles have hope. Jesus continues to heal and to understand family as those who do God's will.

Chapter 13: Third Sermon, *Proclamation of the Kingdom in Parables*

The kingdom of God is in the center of Matthew's gospel and is his central concern. This third sermon is about the kingdom of God or God's reign. The reign of God is explained through parables. The definition of a parable, almost always quoted from C. H. Dodd, is "a metaphor or simile drawn from nature or common life, arresting the hearer by its vividness or strangeness, and leaving the mind in sufficient doubt about its precise application to tease it into active thought."[14]

Jesus tells the disciples and the crowds about the kingdom through parables. The first parable (13:1–8) is about seeds that fall on a path, seeds that fall on rocky ground, and seeds that also fall on good soil. The seeds on good soil flourish and grow like disciples who bear fruit. Another parable compares the kingdom to a woman who mixes yeast into flour to make bread rise. The reign of God expands like growing seeds and rising bread (13:33). The kingdom is also compared to a treasure that is hidden in a field and a pearl of great price. The treasure in the field is found by surprise. The pearl is sought (13:44–45). Glimpses of God's reign may come by surprise or from active seeking.

Chapters 14–17: Third Intervening Block

Between sermons 3 and 4, John the Baptist is executed. Jesus feeds a crowd of five thousand and walks on water. A Canaanite woman helps Jesus see that his ministry extends beyond the lost sheep of Israel (15:21–28). Peter's confession is that Jesus is the Messiah. Jesus tells Peter that he is the rock upon which he will build the church (16:13–20). Jesus is transfigured on the mountain, in a shining, mystical moment that foreshadows future glory (17:1–13).

Chapter 18: Fourth Sermon, *Creating Community*

Matthew cares about community. True greatness in the kingdom is not being childless but childlike, with the ability to trust. Expanding the image of children to "little ones" (18:6), in an ambiguous reference to new converts or to those weak in faith,[15] Matthew's Jesus says that if anyone makes the little one stumble, it would be better to be tossed into the sea and drowned. The parable of God's rejoicing over lost sheep suggests

14. Duling and Perrin, *New Testament*, 603.
15. *HarperCollins Study Bible*, 1890.

joy in retrieving those who stray (vv. 10–13) Forgiveness and discipline in church life are themes in this sermon. Matthew stresses working out wrongdoing within the church. (vv. 15–21) Forgiveness is needed in every generation of human beings. Challenging his audience, Jesus points to a process of forgiveness that is not always quick and easy. He ends this sermon with a beautiful sentence about Christ's presence in community: "For where two or three are gathered in my name, I am there among them"(18:20). This suggests the present aspects of the kingdom that could be experienced in community.

Chapters 19–23: Fourth Intervening Block

After the fourth sermon, Jesus engages in first-century debate about divorce (19:1–12). He blesses children and in the parable of the rich young man, warns about the perils of penny-pinching rather than sharing (19:13–26). Concern about the dangers of wealth ties Jesus to the prophetic and wisdom traditions.

Following Mark's outline, Jesus foretells his death (20:17–19) and cleanses the temple (21:12–13). The question about paying taxes comes from a Pharisee who is not as friendly as his counterpart in Mark. Religious debate heats up. Jesus responds to questions about the resurrection, an issue of the day. The great commandment to love God and neighbor is an interpretive key: "On these two commandments hang all the law and the prophets" (22:40). In a controversy story with the scribes and Pharisees in chapter 23, Jesus distills the weightier matters of law as "justice, mercy and faith" (23:23). (The word *faith* is translated as "integrity" in the Goodspeed translation.[16]) To my mind, these important qualities affect how personal and community ethics unfold in many kinds of community and cultures.

Chapters 24–25: Fifth Sermon, *God Will Have the Last Word*

This fifth sermon is an apocalyptic discourse about God's having the last word in the end. Hearers are challenged to consider the direction or goals that are ultimately the most important. What is the best way to live in the present while waiting for the fullness of the kingdom? Controversy often fuels theological articulation. Two important parables in this sermon are the parable of the bridesmaids (25:1–13) and the parable of the talents (25:14–30). The story of bridesmaids stresses the importance of being ready for the kingdom. The watchword is *watchfulness*. The hint is that Matthew is addressing the problem of Jesus's not coming as soon as

---

16. Goodspeed, trans., *Complete Bible: An American Translation*, 24.

expected. The parable of the talents is about personal gifts used to help God's reign growing on earth in the present time.

Verses 31–46 of chapter 25, which are about the Last Judgment, contain special M material. In this section, people who care for the sick, naked, and imprisoned also care for Christ as perfect embodiment of the Torah: "Truly I tell you, just as you did it to one of the least of these who are members of my family, you did it to me" (25:40). Caring for the needy is application of justice, mercy, and faith. These attributes that, in chapter 23, introduce the theme of caring are further developed in this fifth sermon.

The Great Commission

The baby Jesus, called "Emmanuel" at birth, grows up to be with people in all kinds of trouble and unhappiness. He stands up for those people who are starting their faith journeys and offers assurance to spiritually poor people—assurance that they will be blessed. After his death and resurrection, he tells his disciples, in the translation by Daniel J. Harrington, "Go, make disciples of all the Gentiles, baptizing them in the name of the Father and of the Son and of the Holy Spirit, teaching them to observe all that I have commanded you. And behold I am with you all days until the end of the age" (28:19–20).[17] Jesus promises his presence and proclaims the mission to the Gentiles, that is, to those of us who are not Jews. God will guide and protect the church as it develops over the centuries.

The World in Front of the Text: Two Pictures

Two very different scenes by Marc Chagall may help Christians balance the historical, Jewish Jesus and Jesus as the resurrected Christ, whom most Christians affirm as of the same substance as God. You may find these two images in the book *Crucifixion*, published by Phaidon Press in 2000. Chagall's oil on canvas compares the experiences of the Jewish people of the 1930s to the crucifixion.[18] Jesus suffered as a Jew. The ladder links Jesus's suffering to the earthly persecution of Jesus's and to his descendants who would in time also suffer. Chagall's image reminds Christians that the historical Jesus was a teacher and a Jew.

In Christian mysticism, the ladder is an important image. The thirteenth-century friar and mystic Bonaventure believed that eternal truth itself took on human form in Christ and became a ladder that

---

17. Harrington, *Gospel of Matthew*, 414.
18. Phaidon Press, *Crucifixion*, 209.

restored the first ladder that had been broken in Adam, the first man. For Christians, the spiritual senses are restored through Christ so that the soul like the bride in the Canticle of Canticles can respond to her beloved.[19] Thus, the ladder can both symbolize Jesus linked to all suffering people and also suggest to Christians that Jesus is their connection to the divine like a ladder reaching to God.

A stained glass window, also by Chagall, combined the historical, crucified Jesus and the risen Lord.[20] This crucifixion should not be seen as a christological confession by a Jewish artist but as a gift of empathy and as an evocative image. The glory of the resurrection is implied by the rich, saturated, glorious, jewel tone colors: ruby, emerald green, and sapphire. Angels buoy Christ up in his hour of need.

Jesus's identical substance with God is implied by the sapphire blue under his feet, which is like the sapphire pavement, mentioned in Exodus, that early leaders of Israel saw under God's feet: "Then Moses and Aaron, Nadab and Abihu, and seventy of the elders of Israel went up, and they saw the God of Israel. Under his feet there was something like a pavement of sapphire stone, like the very heaven for clearness" (Exod 24:9–10).

The color blue can be visual poetry and evoke an almost universal human experience of transcendence. God and Jesus as sharing the same substance can be broadly interpreted as God and Jesus having the same essences of beauty and capacity to love sacrificially. Christians who follow Christ's example are not the only people to give sacrificial love. When blue evokes peace and suggests the beauty of holiness, color lifts us out of our selves and intimates transcendent possibilities for self or society.

---

19. Cousins, *Bonaventure*, 32.
20. Phaidon Press, *Crucifixion*, 239.

6

The Gospel according to Luke
Reach Out With Loving Concern Day After Day

Background
Who Was Luke?

LUKE, WHOM we call Luke in regard to tradition, was an anonymous writer and editor. Because he was literary, thoughtful, and calm, he was well suited to his self-assigned task of writing an orderly account so that his patron, Theophilus, would know the truth about the things he had been taught (Luke 1:1–4). In Greek, *Theophilus* means "lover of God." In Acts, which Luke also wrote, the editorial "we" implies that Luke might have been a traveling companion of Paul. In any case, Luke was an educated Greek man who wrote for Gentiles and is traditionally known as the "beloved physician" (Col 4:14). He used Mark, the Q source of sayings, and his own special material. He may have been a "God-fearer." People known as "God-fearers" were attracted to Judaism by the ethical conduct and belief in one God called *ethical monotheism*. In other words, they liked worshipping and behaving well, but circumcision and food rules were not attractive.

Luke wore rose-colored glasses. While Mark's slogan was, "take up your cross," and martyrdom was a distinct possibility in his thought, Luke made a transition to a more inclusive concept of sacrifice. The New English Bible is especially clear: "And to all he said, 'If anyone wishes to be a follower of mine, he must leave self behind; day after day he must take up his cross, and come with me'" (Luke 9:23–24). The phrase "day after day" shifts the emphasis from the certain martyrdom of death to daily sacrificial living.

When Did Luke Write, and Where?

Luke wrote his gospel between 85 and 90 AD. He also wrote Acts, and scholars consider Luke and Acts a two-volume set. Luke most likely wrote to the churches that were influenced by Paul. Southern Greece may have been the place of composition.

Luke verbally pictures Jesus as God's Son, the centerpiece of history, the glory of Israel, and light to the Gentiles. In Luke's understanding, the prophets are in the spiritual history of Israel. Jesus is the centerpiece of that history. The coming of the Holy Spirit that continues into the ongoing future is the third stage of such history. Jesus, in Luke's view, is God's Son from the beginning. His conclusion is implicit in the birth narrative (2:1–20). In Luke, Jesus's identity is proclaimed by angels at his conception, by Jesus himself the first time he speaks (2:49), by God at Jesus's baptism (3:22), and by Paul after the resurrection (Acts 13:32–33).

Simeon was a righteous man who looked forward to the consolation of Israel. The Holy Spirit told him that he would not die before seeing the Lord's Messiah. When Jesus's parents brought him to the temple, Simeon took Jesus in his arms. Simeon praised God saying, "Master, now you are dismissing your servant in peace, according to your word; for my eyes have seen your salvation, which you have prepared in the presence of all peoples, a light for revelation to the Gentiles and for glory to your people Israel" (2:29–32). Devout like Simeon, the boy Jesus at about age twelve told his parents that he must be in his Father's house (2:49).

Themes in the Text or Middle Ground

Luke develops themes in his gospel, so a good way to study Luke is to consider his themes.

Joy

Joy is woven through Luke's writings like a sparkling gold thread that ties the narrative together. John's birth brings joy to his parents (1:14). When John is still in his mother's womb, he leaps for joy when John's mother, Elizabeth, hears Mary's greeting (1:41). Angels tell lowly shepherds bring good news of great joy for all the people (2:10). When the risen Christ appears to the disciples, they are enveloped in joy and wondering (24:41). After Jesus ascends to heaven, the disciples return to Jerusalem with great joy and continue to worship in the temple (24:48–53).

Reversals

In chapter 1, Mary's song foreshadows Jesus's concern for the poor. She sings about reversals or turnarounds: "He has brought down the powerful from their thrones, and lifted up the lowly; he has filled the hungry with good things, and sent the rich away empty" (1:52–53). These verses are poetry inserted into the narrative. When poetry is inside another form of biblical writing, the poetic lines summarize central ideas. Angels and shepherds celebrate Jesus's birth. They foreshadow future joy and reversals from oppression to release. The angels sing and praise God with joy. (There are angels in Matthew's gospel, but the angels in Luke sing better.) Poor shepherds welcome Jesus into the world, and later Jesus will be like a shepherd who welcomes people on the margins. Shepherds and Jesus's mother foreshadow Jesus's passion for the poor, and Jesus himself makes his mission to unfortunate people clear. Luke, an artistic historian with marketing skills, puts the spotlight on Jesus's selecting Scripture. When Jesus returns to Nazareth, he goes to the synagogue and selects a reading from the prophet Isaiah. "The Spirit of the Lord is upon me, because he has anointed me to bring good news to the poor. He has sent me to proclaim release to the captives and recovery of sight to the blind, to let the oppressed go free, to proclaim the year of the Lord's favor" (Luke 4:18–19). This historically plausible and textural image roots Jesus in time and ties him to Israel's prophets and practice. This image works back to Mary's song and points forward to Jesus's ministry.

Luke, like Matthew, features the beatitudes. Matthew spiritualizes these sayings by saying, for example, "poor in spirit" (Matt 5:3). Luke is very aware of economics. His choice of words, or perhaps his variation of Q words, reports Jesus saying, "Blessed are you who are poor, for yours is the kingdom of God" (Luke 6:20). As a social group, the poor are raised to an eschatological category; that is to say, they will have future justice and consolation. Luke scatters the sayings of Jesus throughout his gospel and puts some of the beatitudes in the Sermon on the Plain (6:17–49), whereas Matthew puts them in one block, a large block of teachings in the Sermon on the Mount.

Dangers of Wealth

Luke's concerns for the dangers of wealth are related to his theme of reversals. Idolatry, not just greed, is the issue in the story of the dishonest manager in Luke 16:1–13. The concluding verse is, "No slave can serve two masters; for a slave will either hate the one and love the other, or be devoted to the one and despise the other. You cannot serve God and wealth." The parable of the rich man and Lazarus in 16:19–31 combines the themes of reversals and idolizing of money. (This Lazarus is not the same Lazarus who was raised from the dead.)

Concern For the Lost and Lonely

Luke paints a picture of Jesus as concerned for the lost and lonely and for the outcast and ostracized. You can read his story of the Good Samaritan in Luke 10:25–37. This story evokes not only a broader definition of "neighbor" but also increasing insight about how to be a good one. In Luke's story, the Samaritan, a member of an ostracized group, is the only person to help a man who had been beaten and left for dead at the side of the road. Other people pass by.

Artistic Luke offers counterbalancing images to distinguish how loving God and loving one's neighbor are both the same and different from each other. Luke pairs a kneeling man and a kneeling woman. The Good Samaritan kneels to help his neighbor. A woman of faith, grateful for Jesus's gift of forgiveness, kneels and anoints his feet with ointment (7:36–50). Love of God results in praise and worship as well as in work and service.

In Luke 15 there are three stories that show Jesus's concern for the lost. Luke selects these stories from his manuscript pile (metaphorically speaking) and groups them together in a collection. Taken together they are rich, painterly *impasto*, which means thick, highly textured paint. These stories are the parable of the lost sheep (vv. 1–7), the parable of the lost coin (vv. 8–10), and in the remaining verses the parable of the prodigal son and his elder brother (vv. 11–32). The story of the prodigal son is the most fully developed story and climax of this three-parable set. When I was a senior in high school, our pastor asked the younger people to write a paragraph or two about the older brother's attitude. My short essay was published in the church's newsletter. Of course, it never occurred to me that over forty years later I would insert it into a manuscript:

> In the story of the Prodigal Son, the elder brother does not understand the real reasons for his father's rejoicing. Perhaps he is thinking in terms of "an eye for an eye and a tooth for a tooth" and thinks the merry-making is a strange way to make amends for his brother's mistakes.
>
> The Bible says that the oldest brother was angry. He also seemed jealous of his brother. His anger must have hindered his ability to understand the situation. The eldest son associated his

father's love with a reward for something that was well done. He did not understand that the love was constant. The older brother did not realize that the merrymaking was the father's way of accepting a repentant son.

If the story had continued, perhaps the younger brother would have helped his brother to understand the greatness of his father's love and forgiveness.

The father in the story reflects the love of God the Father. The woman who looks for the lost coin hints at a feminine dimension to God's persistent searching for the lost.

Compassion

Compassion is Jesus's standard of justice in Luke's account. His compassion is summarized in the statement that he healed all (6:19). Jesus advises people to be nonjudgmental: "'Do not judge, and you will not be judged; do not condemn, and you will not be condemned'" (6:37). He wanted his disciples to share in his compassion and taught the measure of compassion that we show will be the measure that we will receive (6:38).

Prayer

In Luke, prayer precedes decisive points. Before choosing the twelve disciples, Jesus goes to the mountain to pray (6:12). When Jesus and his disciples climb a mountain to pray, the disciples see Jesus transformed in clouds and know in their hearts that Jesus is God's Son. You can read this section in Luke 9:28–36. Jesus prays on the Mount of Olives and on the cross. On the mountain he says, "Father if you are willing, remove this cup from me; yet not my will but yours be done" (22:42). In addition to the peace that comes to Jesus from accepting God's will, an angel, according to some ancient authorities, appears to give Jesus strength. On the cross, Jesus the prophet shows the compassion and forgiveness that he had preached in life: "Father, forgive them for they do not know what they are doing" (23:34).

We do not know for certain if Jesus on the cross felt any vindication from his heavenly Father. Yet Luke does give us reason to believe that Jesus trusted God completely and felt peaceful and at one with God. We can deduce that Jesus found God trustworthy because Luke's gospel includes Jesus's words, "Father, into your hands, I commend my spirit" (23:46). Luke either wrote faithful historical fiction based on a deep and accurate understanding of Jesus or he had reliable sources.

Jesus's prayer life was to the glory of God. For Christians he is a model of piety. He must have learned how to pray from his mother, Mary. Mary, as a young woman, praised God for the salvation of the oppressed and lowly (1:47–55). In a contemplative spirit, Mary treasured in her heart the milestones in her son's developing sense of his Father's work (2:51). As a mature woman, Mary was present with the disciples when they devoted themselves to prayer before replacing Judas Iscariot (Acts 1:14).

Salvation

In Luke's gospel, Jesus seeks, saves, and sustains the lost and lonely. In Luke's view, Jesus makes us one with God in two ways:

1. Jesus, as a prophet like Moses, helps us exit from sin's bondage.
2. Jesus, as a second Adam, removes the curse of death.

Heavenly Banquet

The great dinner or heavenly banquet is another of Luke's themes that colors his writing with stronger emphasis on God's universal love than is found in the other two Synoptic Gospels. Luke is convinced that all will be welcome in the kingdom of God. The parable of the great dinner is in Luke 14:15–24.

Word and Sacrament

In Luke, Jesus is a prophet plus. In chapter 4, at Nazareth, the rejected Jesus defines himself by saying, "Truly I tell you, no prophet is accepted in the prophet's hometown" (4:24). Likewise, people describe Jesus as a prophet after he raises a widow's son as did the prophet Elijah before him (7:11–17). For Luke, the earthly Jesus is a prophet and, in addition, the risen Christ who opens the Scriptures and breaks bread is the giver of sacraments.

After the resurrection, Jesus appears to the disciples on the road to Emmaus. The disciples, who at first do not recognize Jesus, talk about the general conversations about Jesus, a prophet mighty in deed (24:19). Then the disciples recognize Jesus in the breaking of the bread: "They said to each other, 'Were not our hearts burning within us while he was talking to us on the road, while he was opening the scriptures to us?'" (24:32). This story about Jesus is sometimes interpreted as a parable about word and sacrament in church life.

Holy Spirit

The Holy Spirit is important in Luke and Acts. The Holy Spirit is present at Jesus's baptism (3:21–22). Empowering Jesus in the wilderness, the Holy Spirit helps him withstand temptations (4:1–13). In chapter 24, verse 49, the risen Jesus, in a postresurrection appearance, promises the disciples what their Father in heaven promised. The promise will turn out to be the Holy Spirit in Acts 1:4–5, 1:8, 2:4, and 2:17–18. In Acts, the Holy Spirit will help the people of God in the earliest assemblies or churches expand from Jerusalem to Rome.

The World in Front of the Text

Simeon's Song of Praise by Art De Gelder, who was influenced by Rembrandt, captured the infant Jesus embraced in prayer and offered in dedication to God by the old Jewish priest, Simeon. In the traditional ceremony of circumcision, good and faithful people surround Jesus. Simeon praises God because he has lived to see a light to the Gentiles and the glory of Israel.

Georges Rouault's painting *Christ in the Outskirts* shows Christ with two small children on the outskirts of a town. In his portrait of Jesus that matches Luke's verbal picture, the artist captures Luke's concern for miserable and marginal people. Both of these paintings may be found in *Sister Wendy's 1000 Masterpieces: Sister Wendy Beckett's Selection of the Greatest Paintings in Western Art*.[1] Many public libraries will have Sister Wendy's books.

How can you help someone known or unknown to you who is lonely, yearning for inclusion, hungry, or hurting?

---

1. Beckett, *Sister Wendy's 1000 Masterpieces*, 165, 401.

7

The Acts of the Apostles
Trust in the Holy Spirit and Spread the Word

Background
What Is Acts?

LUKE AND Acts are a two-volume set by an anonymous Gentile Christian. Evidence that they were written by the same person includes uniform style, shared ideas, and dedication to Theophilus. Luke's main job was theological storyteller, and he moonlighted as an historian with a special interest in salvation history. The underlying assumption of salvation historians, including Luke and Paul, is that God's purposes are working out in history. God is guiding history through God's Spirit. As a theological historian, Luke was not concerned for exact detail. However, he roots his stories and sermons in history. There may be something to be said for a pre-Enlightenment view that accepts the Bible as a reliable narrative, and if there are legends mixed in, it is no big deal. If you wish, relax and read this book as purely historical fiction. Your mind may be freed up to enjoy the power of poetry and the sustenance of symbol. One of my college professors said that fiction is a lie that tells you more about the truth than the truth does. I often contemplate John Keats's understanding of imagination as an important organ of perception.

Acts is also an adventure story with a theological message. The book of Luke tells the story of Jesus from birth to death to resurrection. Acts continues the narrative from Jesus's ascension to Paul's imprisonment in Rome. Contemporary readers will find two main parts of the story:

1. The church starts.
2. The church spreads.

Luke may have been a traveling companion of Paul or the editorial "we" may be a literary device that was common at the time. In any case,

Acts is the story of how Paul and other apostles carried on their mission to the Gentiles. The Holy Spirit empowered and guided all the servants of the Word. The main character, Paul, was a devout Jew who changed his mind about the emerging Jewish Christian sect. Maps of the missionary journeys are reconstructions and approximations. I've never found them appealing and have not included any in this book.

When Was Acts Written?

Acts was written around 85–90 AD outside of Palestine.

Why Was Acts Written?

Luke wanted to show "how the word of the Lord grew" (19:20), and how early Christianity spread from Jerusalem to Rome.

The Text
Color Words

Luke's names for God would appeal to philosophical Greeks who were attracted to ethical monotheism. God is called "Author of Life" (3:15) and "Holy and Righteous One" (3:14).

Perspective

Luke's perspective is that by the power of the Holy Spirit the Gospel message will spread throughout the world. Artist Luke sketches the lengthening timeline of the Christian movement into Greek culture. The certainty of the growth of the Christian movement was expressed well by the divinity school professor of my college professor. Edgar J. Goodspeed wrote: "The thread of the narrative is no mere biography but the providential fashion in which the gospel had groped its way out of Judaism into widening circles—Roman and Ethiopian, proselyte and Samaritan—until at length, in Antioch, the apostles began to preach to Greeks with no Jewish preparation and then to the whole Mediterranean world. No man plans it, not even the apostles. It happened involuntarily but inevitably, in an almost casual way, by human contacts."[1]

---

1. Goodspeed, *Introduction to the New Testament*, 186–87.

Line

Although Acts is a travel story featuring the acts of God and actions of people, there are rest areas on the way. Despite death and debris from intense religious debates, there are places of refreshment and reflective moments in speeches and prayers.

"The Way" is a metaphor for the formative or earliest Christian church and also suggests the twists and turns of Paul's trips. In Acts, those who walk in Jesus's way find their way with the guidance of the Holy Spirit, with the help of angels, and with the empowerment of the Spirit that boosted boldness.

As more people join the way, requirements of faith are simplified, and understanding of God 's grace and power expands. People known as "God-fearers," who were already attracted to Jewish beliefs in one God and ethical living, but who found some requirements off-putting, signed up, as did other people in the ancient world who were convinced by signs and wonders, sermons and stories. Take a fast-paced survey through my chapter-by-chapter postcard jottings from Paul's journey.

The Church Starts

Chapter 1   After his resurrection but before his ascension, Jesus appears to his apostles. Luke, who liked to find the right words, uses an especially strong Greek word for "proofs" of Jesus's resurrection (v. 3). At the start of his spiritualized travel history, Luke's choice of words states his most basic value, which is the power of Christ over death. After promising baptism by the Holy Spirit and power to witness to the ends of the earth, Jesus ascends into heaven (vv. 8–9). Guided by prayer and by casting lots, the apostles choose Matthias to replace Judas (vv. 24–26).

Chapter 2   Happy Birthday, Church. Tongues of fire touch the heads of all the gathered people with the Holy Spirit that transcends languages and cultures. Peter explains that people are not drunk with wine but are fulfilling the words of the Old Testament prophet Joel who said that God will pour out his spirit, that sons and daughters will prophecy, that young man shall see visions and old men shall dream (vv. 1–21). Peter preaches his most basic conviction that the power of death cannot hold Jesus (v. 24). Believers have all things in common (2:44). They devote themselves to the apostles' teachings, fellowship, breaking bread and praying together (vv. 46–47).

Chapter 3   Peter and John tell a lame man to walk (vv. 6–7). Faith flows into praise. Faith and trust start to open up for Gentiles as well as Jews.

Chapter 4	Sadducees, who do not believe in the resurrection from the dead, have Peter and John arrested (vv. 2–3). Peter and John are released and visit supportive friends. This is a time of grace and sharing. There is not one needy person in this communal gathering.
Chapter 5	Ananias and his wife, Sapphira, do not share as they have promised and are struck down (v. 5), which may be a dramatic way of saying their lies caused them to self-destruct. More people join the Christian movement that threatens the status quo. Gamaliel, a Pharisee and teacher of the Law, suggests leaving the apostles alone because if their plans are of human origin the plans will not last, but that if the apostles' goals are from God, then who wants to be found fighting against God (vv. 34–39)? Most likely, he was the same Gamaliel who was Paul's teacher.
Chapter 6	Church administrators are appointed to run the church's meals program. Stephen, full of grace and power, does great wonders (v. 8).
Chapter 7	After summarizing the spiritual history of the Israelite people, Stephen concludes that God is bigger than the temple or human institutions (7:48–50). His insight is not well received, and he is stoned to death. In the spirit of Luke's compassionate Jesus, Stephen prays, "Lord Jesus, receive my spirit," and asks that the sin of his killers will not be held against them (vv. 58–60).
Chapter 8	Devout men bury Stephen (v. 2). Saul actively persecutes the church. Simon, who is a magician, sees real miracles taking place. The high contrast between magic and miracle is an artistic device that highlights the power of faith. Philip explains to a man from Ethiopia that Jesus is like the sheep led to the slaughter in the Old Testament book of Isaiah (vv. 31–33).
Chapter 9	Saul, later called Paul, has a life-altering experience. Approaching Damascus, he is blinded by a heavenly light and hears Jesus asking him, why is he, Saul, persecuting Jesus? (9: 3–5). Meanwhile the risen Christ tells Ananias (not the one who died in chapter 5) to go to Saul and to put his hands on Saul's eyes to heal them. Paul sees, and changes his mind about the new religious movement. Through revelation from religious experience, Saul comes to understand that he is chosen to bring Jesus before the Gentiles. Changed, chosen, and called, Saul starts to open the Gentile mission that will bring knowledge of God's love to Greek or Hellenist people and all people who are not Jewish (v. 29). Peter heals Tabitha, whose name in Greek is Dorcas. She had made clothes for people, and news of her healing spreads through the outreach of sewing circles. More people come to believe in Jesus and the Way.

Chapter 10	As an artistic writer, Luke does theology through story writing. Peter's religious experience in the center of Acts is the core insight that helps him to challenge customs that honor boundaries imposed by strict observance of dietary laws and to consider more inclusive fellowship. Cornelius, a devout man who believed in God, prayed constantly. He had a vision of an angel who told him to send to Joppa for Simon, also known as Peter. While the men are on their way to fetch Peter, Peter goes up on a roof to pray. He is hungry and falls into a trance. In this altered state he sees a sheet filled with animals. A voice tells him to eat from the sheet. He thinks it best to not eat but then hears a voice telling him that what God made must not be called profane (v.15). Peter thinks about the vision. The spirit informs him that the men are looking for him. He first invites in those who sought him, and then he travels to Joppa with them. Peter is quite willing to meet with Cornelius, who was a Gentile, because Peter had already been told not to call anyone unclean or profane. Cornelius tells Peter about his vision that assured him his prayers had been answered and to send for Peter (vv. 30–32). Thus, Peter realizes that anyone who does what is right is acceptable to God, and that the Holy Spirit has been poured out even on the Gentiles (v. 44). Revelation came through personal experience that freed Peter to accept people who did not observe all the food regulations.
Chapter 11	The story is retold with the conclusion that God has given even to the Gentiles the repentance that leads to life. Barnabas takes Saul to Antioch, and for a year they meet with the people in Antioch, where the disciples are first called Christians (v. 26).
Chapter 12	Peter is imprisoned and the church prays for him. An angel frees Peter, and the word spreads.

The Church Spreads

Chapter 13	Through the Holy Spirit, the church at Antioch knows that Barnabas and Saul, now often called Paul, were called to travel. After twists and turns in the journey, Paul summarizes his evolving understanding of God's commands: "I have set you to be a light for the Gentiles, so that you may bring salvation to the ends of the earth" (v. 47). As the Gentile mission grows, the disciples are filled with joy and the Holy Spirit.
Chapter 14	Rest area: After Paul heals a man who had never walked, he has to convince people that he is a mortal, not a god. He speaks of the past, when the Greek people and other non-Jews did not know the one God. He says that God did not leave himself without a wit-

ness in doing good. As signs of God doing good things, Luke cites rain from heaven and fruitful seasons, and also God's filling people with food and hearts with joy (v. 17). One can imagine poetic Luke reflecting upon these signs of God's goodwill throughout his life. These happy aspects of life universally evoke gratitude. Luke, who has the talent to universalize, ends this chapter with reflections about the door of faith for the Gentiles.

Chapter 15 Circumcision is reinterpreted as cleansing of the heart (v. 9). An important church council meeting in Jerusalem declares circumcision unnecessary by maintaining that "we should not trouble those Gentiles who are turning to God" (v. 19). Food laws are modified so that those requirements would not be burdensome to new converts (vv. 28–29). Personal religious experience supporting more inclusive fellowship was distilled and translated into policy. Barnabas and Paul part company, Paul and Silas set out through Syria and Cilicia on a trip, with the goal of strengthening churches (vv. 40–41).

Chapter 16 Timothy joins Paul and Silas on the journey. In Macedonia, Lydia, who already worshipped God, joins the Christian movement (vv. 14–15). She is a successful businesswoman who trades in purple cloth. Perhaps Luke tells this story to suggest that Christianity appealed to successful people as well as to people on the margins of life, whom he emphasized in his gospel. A slave girl recognizes Paul and Silas as slaves of the "Most High God" (v. 17). Whether this story is a literary device of a slave understanding slaves of a different sort, or whether this story is bedrock historical fact, poetic Luke accurately portrays Paul and Silas. Paul and Silas interfere with a fortune-telling business, which does not please businesspeople. Paul and Silas go to jail but are freed by an earthquake. The jailer becomes a believer (vv. 25–34).

Chapter 17 Paul goes to Athens, awaiting Silas and Timothy. While there, he is inspired to be diplomatic and to draw upon his knowledge of poetry. He tells the Athenians that he can see that they are religious (v. 22). He suggests that an altar inscription reading, "to an unknown God" names the God who made the world and everything in it (vv. 23–25). The main point of Paul's proclamation here is that people, made in the image of God, should not worship idols. Speaking philosophically, Paul says, "For 'In him we live and move and have our being'; as even some of your own poets have said, 'For we too are his offspring'" (v. 28).

Chapter 18 Paul leaves Athens and goes to Corinth to stay with Aquila and his wife, Priscilla. After some opposition in Corinth, Paul intensi-

PART ONE: THE GOSPEL AND GROWING PROCLAMATION

fies his commitment to the Gentile mission. After more travel, he comes to Ephesus and teaches Apollos, who is eloquent and knowledgeable about the new Christian religion (vv. 24–28).

Chapter 19   In Ephesus, Paul weakens the local economy by criticizing the manufacturing of silver idols. A wise town clerk tells people to cool down, because Paul has not broken the law or done something horrible such as robbing temples (vv. 35–41).

Chapter 20   Paul sets out for Greece. While Paul is talking to people, a young man listening dozes off and falls out of the window. He recovers (vv. 9–11). (Apparently, then as now, putting people to sleep is sometimes an occupational hazard for preachers. This seemingly inconsequential detail adds a sense of believability and even comic relief to Luke's artful account.) Back on a ship, Paul continues the journey, and from Miletus Paul sends a message asking the elders of the Ephesian church to meet him. Speaking to the elders, Paul said that he did not count his life of any value to himself; he simply wanted to finish his course and his ministry (v. 24).

Chapter 21   Paul and crew get back into the boat and sail on to Rhodes, and eventually to Jerusalem. Bringing Greeks into the Jerusalem temple did not increase Paul's popularity with people of the established religion. The tribune that arrests Paul realizes that Paul is not the Egyptian who had stirred up a revolt (v. 38). Paul asks for permission to speak to the people.

Chapter 22   Paul speaks in Hebrew (v. 2) and is listened to, up to the point when he says that God has sent him to the Gentiles. Having been born a Roman citizen, however, Paul has some legal protection.

Chapter 23   Speaking to a religious council that is meeting at the request of the Roman tribune, Paul says that he is on trial for hope in the resurrection (v. 6). Thus, he sets up a fight between the Sadducees (who do not believe resurrection from the dead) and the Pharisees (who, like the emerging Christian movement, do believe in resurrection). Paul knows, as God told him, that he would bear witness in Rome (v. 11). Paul's nephew overcomes a plot against Paul, and the tribune (vv. 16–22) protects Paul. Paul is sent to Felix, governor in Caesarea.

Chapter 24   When Festus succeeds Felix in Caesarea, Felix, who had been interested in learning about the Way and possible payoffs, leaves Paul in prison.

Chapter 25   Festus tells Paul that because Paul has appealed to the emperor, he will go to the emperor.

Chapter 26	Paul speaks for himself and tells the story of his experience on the road to Damascus. He reiterates the importance of proclamation of light to the Gentiles. King Agrippa tells Festus that if Paul had not appealed to the emperor, he could have been freed (v. 32).
Chapter 27	Paul is sent on a boat to Italy with other prisoners. A northeaster, which is an intense storm, blows up. An angel tells Paul that since he must stand before the emperor, safety will be granted to all on board. Paul tells the men to keep up their courage, for he has faith in God. Eating together in a way that echoes the Eucharist; the prisoners regain strength (vv. 33–38). After their ship strikes a reef, the prisoners are told to swim for shore. All are brought to safety.
Chapter 28	This concluding chapter presents a vista of beauty and rest as well as a summary of the end and meaning of Paul's life. Paul and the prisoners land on the island known as Malta, where the natives show them unusual kindness. When Paul shakes off a poisonous snake, the natives are impressed and think that Paul is a god (v. 6). A leading man named Publius hospitably entertains Paul and the others. His father is sick, so Paul visits this sick man and heals him. Many people on the island are cured, and, therefore, when the time comes for Paul and the crew to sail again, the grateful people stock the ship with provisions (v. 10). After arriving in Rome, Paul is held with a jailer in a kind of house arrest but continues his preaching ministry. As the book of Acts concludes, Paul says, "Let it be known to you then that this salvation of God has been sent to the Gentiles; they will listen" (28:28). The story ends with an open-ended note because we do not know for certain that Paul died in prison. In any case, he rounds out his life doing what he did best, which was preaching the good news of God's love for all, revealed in Jesus the Christ.

The World in Front of the Text

Pentecost, a picture by Emil Nolde, captures the joy and unity at Pentecost. Clasped hands symbolize the extension of the hand of fellowship. This image can be found in many books about contemporary art.

Expanding the metaphor of "the Way" beyond the text into the present, we may understand "the way" as a symbol of finding the paths of our own spiritual journeys. There are dangers that threaten our ability to trust and follow God and Christ or Life and the Source of Life looking for us. Yet there are vistas of beauty, renewal and experiences of human kindness on the journey. Whether you are religious or not, can you identify the happy times in church or other places where you experience joy and renewal?

Part Two

The Community of the Word

8

The Gospel according to John
God so Loved the World

Background
Who Was John?

MOST LIKELY, the primary author of the Gospel of John as suggested from the contents was "one who regarded himself in the tradition of the disciple whom Jesus loved"[1] or, put more simply, a Jewish Christian who was a student of the beloved disciple (this student is hereafter called John). Featured in John's gospel, the beloved disciple is an anonymous person who became a model follower. In the last chapter of the Gospel, he is credited with writing many things in it. Most conclude that he was responsible for passing on traditions to the primary author of John. An editor, who is sometimes called the ecclesiastical redactor, followed the primary author. This editor, as his title implies, added duplicate and previously omitted material to the text as well as church traditions.[2] For example, John 3:31–36 seem to be duplicated in John 3:7, 3:11–13, and 3:15–18. The author-editor may not have wanted to lose variations and could not store duplicate material on a CD-ROM. The image of Jesus as bread of life or revelation in John 6:35 may have been rounded out with Eucharistic implications in 6:51–58.

What Did John and His Editors Write?

John and his editors wrote a poetic and theological gospel that is different from Matthew, Mark, and Luke in style and content. During my college days, forty years ago, most scholars did not think that John was based on much historical fact. Yet John's theological writings flow from the witness

1. Brown, *Introduction to The New Testament*, 334.
2. Ibid., 367.

of John the Baptist, who is a concrete historical figure. Today the emphasis has shifted, and more scholars believe that John had some very early sources that were something like Mark's sources, as well as some other forms that were less complete yet still similar to the forms that Luke used. A pre-Markan source that both Mark and John might have used is a passion and resurrection source. Luke and John might have had a source of stories that included different versions of the story about a woman who wipes Jesus's feet with her hair.[3]

Where Was the Gospel of John Written?

John may have written in Ephesus. Others say Syria.

When Was the Gospel of John Written?

John was written around 90 AD.

Why and to Whom Was the Gospel of John Written?

One of the author's intentions is stated near the end of his Gospel: "Now Jesus did many other signs in the presence of his disciples, which are not written in this book. But these are written so that you may come to believe that Jesus is the Messiah, the Son of God, and that through believing you may have life in his name" (20:30–31). For John, faith in Jesus is always faith in God the Father (12:44).

Despite the words, "come to believe," this Gospel likely was not intended to be a missionary tract according to Fr. Daniel J. Harrington, SJ, in his book *Who Is Jesus? Why Is He Important?* More likely, this gospel was authored to help believers adjust to life outside of the synagogue.[4]

There are conflicting nuances of thought in the Gospel of John. John wrote with the generous hint that Divine Wisdom existed before the physical incarnation of Jesus and is present in the continual guidance of the Advocate. Therefore, Wisdom transcends even the Bible? So why would John strongly imply that there is only one way to God? John's audience and situation affected his theology. Perspective comes through consideration of community needs and context.

John's writing was most likely authored to help Jewish Christians understand their spiritual life outside of the synagogue. John's community needed to know who Jesus was for them. Imagine the predicament of

---

3. Duling and Perrin, *New Testament*, 414–15.
4. Harrington, *Who Is Jesus?* 61.

the Jews who had been expelled from their synagogue for following Jesus. The people who were asked to leave may even have been included in a benediction prayer against the heretics, a prayer that arose in the rabbinical tradition between 80 and 90 AD. They had been faithful in worship and practice all their lives. Yet they had been a bit different for many years. Perhaps middle-aged parents told their young adult children that their great-grandfathers and grandmothers had said there was no earthly reason for Jesus to have been put to death. The Romans did not have a strong legal case. Jesus was a good Jew who opened up an understanding of righteous living and the love of God to many people—rich and poor, Jewish and non-Jewish.

The Jews who were interested in the teachings of Jesus could not go back to their synagogue. They had beliefs that set them apart from other Jews. In a veiled reference to Exodus 33:17–23 (when Moses had wanted to see God's glory but could only see God's shadow), John's reflection on the significance of Jesus for the community states, "No one has ever seen God. It is God the only Son, who is close to the Father's heart, who had made him known" (1:18). The Jews who were asked to leave the synagogue believed that Jesus was heavenly in origin and thus superior to both John the Baptist and Moses. Their conclusion was that divine revelation is vested in Jesus. God loves the Son. Belief in the Son means eternal life (3:31–36). The Jews at odds with the authorities believed that Jesus called God his Father and thereby made himself equal with God (5:18). Naturally, those in authority thought the budding Christians were giving up Jewish monotheism of belief in one God and making a second God out of Jesus. Jews in control of the synagogue thought Moses was the most important person in Jesus's background. To simplify and paraphrase Raymond E. Brown, Jews who were asked to leave stressed Divine Wisdom as the background of Jesus.[5] "The Wisdom of God had become human. That is the basic theological affirmation of John's Gospel."[6] The new Christian community, in its struggles against the synagogue authorities, increasingly came to see that Jesus was from God (9:1–41). Their central confession that forced separation is that Jesus is the Messiah (9:22). Coming to grips with how you understand Jesus is part of John's theology.

The persecuted community was like the blind man whose spiritual sight increased as his faith in Jesus grew (9:1–41). This man, once blind, was a new disciple who was fearless, and who helped new Christians to have courage as they faced interrogation. Thus, the story of the blind man

5. Brown, *Introduction to the New Testament*, 374–75.
6. Harrington, *Who is Jesus?* 62.

in chapter 9 is about an individual and also about the social conflict that John's community faced. The Jews who broke away and those who stayed in the conservative synagogue naturally did not get along. Rancor and revilement raged. Now there was no turning back from the developing Christian movement that was the best choice for Jewish Christians in the ancient world.

Adopting the many gods in popular Roman and Greek religions was not an option for followers of Jesus. Going to a city center to study philosophers like Plato (who, unlike the common people, believed in eternal realities and something very close to the Jewish idea of one God) was also not possible. Jewish Christians were rooted in Palestine, where people tended sheep, baked bread, grew grapevines in sacred soil, and drew life-giving water around a communal well. Married people with families simply could not join with the monks who lived by the Dead Sea and who thought, as did the expelled Jews, in terms of battles between the forces of darkness and light.

Now even hopes for a rebuilt temple lost appeal for followers of Jesus. There was no choice. The only possible way for the members of John's community to connect with God was through Jesus. Eventually, there would be a new kind of temple as people joined together in a new body of mutual regard and belief in God as Word and Wisdom clarified in Jesus. People in the Johannine community experienced new life and found nourishment in Jesus, who was for them the bread of life.

Distinctive Features of the Text
Manner of Speech

In this gospel, Jesus does not speak in parables and rarely mentions the kingdom of God. In contrast to the Synoptic Gospels' focus on the reign of God, John's emphasis is on joy made complete, and on an earthly foretaste of eternal life through believing (5:24). "There is a strong emphasis on the present or realized dimension of eternal life."[7] In John's reflective writing style, monologues and dialogues follow actions and signs. The words of Jesus, sometimes placed in his mouth by wise editors, are meditations of the early church about the significance of Jesus for the Johannine community. In John, Jesus speaks in both long discourses and short iconic statements. Chapter 10, about Jesus the Good Shepherd, provides an example of both a long explanation and a pithy sentence. Verses 1–21 are the

7. Harrington, *How to Read the Gospels*, 43.

long statement. The short sentence that is an iconic statement is, "I am the good shepherd" (10:11). You can easily imagine a shepherd as a computer symbol, a kind of icon. People do not talk in normal conversation like Jesus does in John. So the style of discourse is a big hint that this gospel is a theological writing. In keeping with the rules for writing in the ancient world, the authors and editor put words into Jesus's mouth that he should or would have said to John's readers. As a theological masterpiece, the Gospel of John explains who Jesus is for John's community.

When I was in college in the 1960s, the Gospel of John was thought to be completely Hellenistic, or Greek, in style and content. Somehow we did not notice the visual images of sheep, bread, wine, and vines that suggest the rural environment of Palestine. After the discovery of the Dead Sea Scrolls, it was clearer that Jesus had some shared vocabulary and thought with members of the Dead Sea community.[8] Thus, it appears that the dualism of dark and light and John's artistic style of modeling in dark and light is not purely Greek but Palestinian as well, because the Dead Sea Scrolls from the Palestinian region feature these same contrasts. Raymond E. Brown says that the resemblance and thought between the Dead Sea Scrolls and John should banish the idea that the Johannine tradition could not have developed on Palestinian soil.[9]

Spiritual Chiaroscuro

The most pronounced artistic quality of John's text is verbal modeling in light and dark, in black and white. The artistic term for modeled light and dark is *chiaroscuro* (pronounced kee-a-row-skyu-ro). This Italian word literally means "light-dark." There is spiritual chiaroscuro in John's gospel. Likewise, artists throughout the centuries have picked up on the symbolism of dark and light in John's gospel.

Belief That Jesus Is Preexistent

In John, Jesus is conscious of preexistence with God.

Public Ministry in Jerusalem

According to John, Jesus' public ministry was mainly in Jerusalem rather than Galilee. He goes to Jerusalem three times instead of just once as he does in the other Gospels.

---

8. *Harper's Bible Commentary*, 1045.
9. Brown, *Introduction to the New testament*, 373.

Anger Foreshadowing of the Future

In John's story, the cleansing of the temple occurs at the start of Jesus's ministry rather than towards the end as in the Synoptics. Jesus is angrier in John's account of the temple cleansing than he is in the other Gospels. His anger foreshadows the end of his life. Jesus will be whipped and the temple of his body destroyed before a three-day interval and climatic moment of resurrection.

Time of the Last Supper

In the Synoptic Gospels, the Last Supper was a Passover meal. John does not agree, and paints a picture of the Last Supper before the Passover, a pre-Passover meal. This is an important distinction because by implication Jesus in John is the paschal or sacrificial lamb. The death of the Lamb of God at the same time as the killing of the Passover lamb is a brilliant storytelling device that may or may not be factual, but for Christians conveys an abiding truth about Jesus's sacrificial love as the Lamb of God. Together the Gospels' contrasting accounts of the Last Supper give a complete picture of Jesus as both an observant Jew and sacrificial lamb.

Meaning of Jesus's Birth

Matthew and Luke tell stories about Jesus's birth. John does not have a birth story. However, John draws out the meaning of Jesus's birth in one most excellent sentence: "The light shines in the darkness, and the darkness did not overcome it" (1:5).

Textured Picture of the Paraclete

John's picture of the Paraclete or Counselor is a richly textured portrait. Texture comes from the varied roles that the Advocate has in relating to the people of God. The Paraclete imports the indwelling life of God and has the following job description: pastoral counselor and advocate, teacher and witness, defendant and guidance counselor.

In John's understanding, Jesus will ask God to send the Counselor so that Christians will not be lonely. "If you love me, you will keep my commandments. And I will ask the Father, and he will give you another Advocate, to be with you forever" (14:15–16).

The Counselor will also be a teacher who will remind believers of everything Jesus said. "But the Advocate, the Holy Spirit, whom the Father will send in my name, will teach you everything, and remind you of all that I have said to you" (14:26).

As witness, the Counselor will testify about Jesus in the Spirit of Truth (15:26). Being a witness to life gone wrong in the world (16:7–11) is also a gift of the Holy Spirit. As witness to sin, the Counselor is Defendant of the righteous. There is hope for vindication. Like a wise guidance counselor, the Counselor will guide Jesus's followers into truth as they journey through life (16:12–15).

The Two-Part Line of the Text

The two-part line in John is an artistic and organizational feature of the text. Let us explore the text in the middle ground through consideration of lines that carry signs, stories and symbolic word images of Jesus.

John's gospel is divided into two parts that follow the Prologue. The first part, or line, of stories, called "the Book of Signs," depicts miracles and shows Jesus drawing many kinds of people to him. Signs point to deeper meanings of Jesus for Christians. In the second part, or line of development, known as "the Book of Glory," Jesus instructs his disciples and glorifies God by finishing his earthly work.

The Prologue, which is a poetic hymn, introduces Jesus as the incarnate Word in the first five verses of John's Gospel:

> In the beginning was the Word, and the Word was with God, and the Word was God. He was in the beginning with God. All things came into being through him, and without him not one thing came into being. What has come into being in him was life, and the life was the light of all people. (1:1–5)

Part 1: The Book of Signs

In the "Book of Signs" (John 1:19–12:50), Jesus is revealed through different actions and titles. John shares his vision of a dove descending upon Jesus at his baptism. John understands the dove to signify that Jesus will baptize by the Holy Spirit. John's composition conveys the spirit of a legal atmosphere in which the Jews who favored the new Jesus program had to defend themselves when testifying that Jesus is the Son of God (1:34). After Nathanael, whom Jesus sees as "an Israelite in whom there is no deceit," recognizes Jesus as the Son of God and King of Israel, Jesus speaks of himself in metaphorical words that echo language from the story of Jacob's ladder in the Old Testament: "And he said to them, 'Very truly, I tell you, you will see heaven opened and the angels of God ascending and descending upon the Son of Man'" (1:51). The implicit image of a ladder suggests that Jesus will connect earth and heaven.

In John chapter 2, Jesus changes water into wine at a wedding and cleanses the Temple. This story introduces the theme of confrontation. In chapter 3, under the darkness of night that symbolizes a lack of comprehension about Jesus, Nicodemus, educated but not enlightened, takes the phrase "born again" literally rather than spiritually (v. 4). Assurance of eternal life is a gift that is summed up in perhaps the most favorite verse in the New Testament, John 3:16: "For God so loved the world that he gave his only Son, so that everyone who believes in him may not perish but may have eternal life." Both John the Baptist and Jesus baptize people, but the Baptist stresses that he is less important than is Jesus. He refers to himself as "the friend of the bridegroom" (v. 29). The role of the friend is to rejoice in the joy and purity of the marriage. Thus Jesus's marriage to Christian community is pure, holy, and joyful.

In chapter 4, Jesus offers living water to a Samaritan woman (vv. 3–15). Living water is a poetic metaphor for refreshment and renewal. Samaritans were outsiders (v. 9), but the Samaritan woman's perception was that Jesus might be the Messiah (v. 29). She has an expectant faith that contrasts with Nicodemus's in chapter 3. Her attitude is openness to Jesus as the Christ and to the future when worshippers would worship in spirit and truth: "God is spirit, and those who worship him must worship in spirit and truth" (v. 24). Then Jesus tells his disciples that his food or spiritual nourishment is to do the will of God by completing God's work (v. 34).

In chapter 5, Jesus heals with authority on the Sabbath and thus shows strength and power. Jesus does not testify about himself but lets his works and his heavenly Father affirm him.

The image of bread, prominent in chapter 6, must have been appealing especially to the Samaritans who, like Moses, worshipped on a mountain. Jesus is revealed as the new Moses, the Bread of Life, which sustains like Old Testament manna had in the wilderness. "Jesus said to them, 'I am the bread of life. Whoever comes to me will never be hungry, and whoever believes in me will never be thirsty'" (v. 35). In John, Jesus fulfills festivals. Passover was a very important festival in the history of John's community. For John's emerging congregation, Jesus became fulfillment of this festival because he came to be understood as the Bread of Life that sustains the people of God. The symbol of bread has Eucharistic overtones. "Those who eat my flesh and drink my blood abide in me and I in them . . . This is the bread that came down from heaven, not like that which your ancestors ate . . . But the one who eats this bread will live forever" (vv. 56–58).

In chapter 7, on the last day of the Feast of Tabernacles, Jesus says that anyone who is thirsty can come to him and living water will flow from believers' hearts. In chapter 8, Jesus shows compassion for a woman caught in adultery. His wise advice is that anyone without sin should cast the first stone. Whether the voice of the early church or a belief in the heart of Christ, the iconic statement is "I am the light of the world" (v. 12). For the people in John's community, truth was vested in Jesus, and old traditions took on new meanings. Changes in perspective were liberation for them: "So if the Son makes you free, you will be free indeed" (v. 36).

Chapter 9 is a powerful account, in both poetry and prose, of a blind man's unfolding faith in Jesus. A man who was born blind becomes able to see both physically and spiritually. The movement in the story of the blind man's increasing insight is from understanding Jesus as a prophet (v. 17) to experiencing Jesus as a healer from God (vv. 30–34) to seeing Jesus as Lord (v. 38). When the Pharisees first asked the blind man for his assessment of Jesus the blind man said that Jesus is a prophet. When asked if Jesus was a sinner the blind man, speaking in poetic prose, said, "One thing I do know, that though I was blind, now I see" (v. 25). Then the blind man shares his conviction that if Jesus who healed him was not from God he could do nothing (9:33). Finally in a revelatory conversation with Jesus that blind man knows Jesus as Lord. We can imagine that other people in John's community had a similar development of thought and piety. Slowly, stories about Jesus become double stories about both Jesus and the emerging church. In chapter 10, Jesus is the Good Shepherd who is willing to give his life for his flock: "The good shepherd lays down his life for the sheep" (v. 11). "I am the good shepherd. I know my own and my own know me" (v.14).

In chapter 11, the iconic statement of a central idea is, "I am the resurrection and the life" (v. 25). Jesus raises Lazarus and tells their friends to "unbind him, and to let him go" (v. 44). The first people to hear this story must have been reminded of the Old Testament story of Abraham and Isaac. Abraham misunderstood God's command and almost sacrificed his son before an angel stayed Abraham's hand, and he unbound Isaac. The unbinding reinforces the theme of being set free. Chapter 12 contains two stories (Mary's anointing Jesus and Jesus's entry into Jerusalem) and a summary of his teachings.

Part 2: The Book of Glory

The "Book of Glory" is John chapters 13–20. In the Book of Glory, as its title implies, Jesus glorifies God by finishing his earthly work and returning to the Father through his passion, death, and resurrection.

When someone knows that he or she will soon die, that person might put together meaningful rituals with family and friends. A terminally ill person might also make a video or scrapbook of her life or write an essay explaining his outlook on living and dying. Some people might also write a prayer.

Jesus does a variation on all these things as recorded in John 13–17. In chapter 13, Jesus washes the feet of the disciples in a meaningful ritual (vv. 2–5) and foretells his betrayal.

He gives the new commandment that we love one another:

> I give you a new commandment that you love one another. Just as I have loved you, you should love one another. By this everyone will know that you are my disciples, if you have love for one another. (vv. 34–35)

Chapters 14–16 are Jesus's farewell address. The highlight of chapter 14 is Jesus's promise not to leave his followers orphaned. He tells us that we should not be afraid nor let our hearts be troubled. Jesus promises to ask God to send the Holy Spirit—the Paraclate or Advocate. In short, Jesus promises the peace that is at the center of Israel's hope. In chapter 15, Jesus describes himself as the true vine. Bearing fruit glorifies the Father. The world's hatred is acknowledged, although recognition of widespread distaste for the newly formed community does not mean that God does not love the world. Chapter 16 contains the promise that sorrow will be turned into joy. Jesus concludes by assuring the disciples that he is not alone, because God the Father is with him. The greatest love is laying down one's life for a friend.

In chapter 17, Jesus prays for his disciples in a prayer that is kind of earthly ascension of the Son to the Father, a heightened experience of lifting heart and soul to God. Jesus speaks of eternal life: "And this is eternal life, that they may know you, the only true God, and Jesus Christ whom you have sent. I glorified you on earth by finishing the work that you gave me to do" (vv. 3–4). This prayer is Jesus's offering of his life to complete God's work. Thus, Jesus lived and would soon die to the glory of God. He also prays for the safeguarding of the faith community and for the union of Father and Son with community so "they may all be one" (v. 21).

The Gospel according to John

In chapter 18, Jesus is arrested. Caiaphas, the high priest, had advised that it was better to have one person die for the people (v.14). Given that, in the views of many Christians, Jesus died for the sake of all people, readers will not miss the irony of Caiaphas's statement.

Jesus appears before the high priest for questioning. Peter denies Jesus. Jesus appears before Pilate; Jesus tells Pilate that his (Jesus's) kingdom is not of this world (v. 36). Chapter 19 is the heart of the passion story. John details the flogging, and the crucifixion between two others. John movingly recounts Jesus's giving up his spirit to God. Jesus is buried according to the burial customs of the Jews.

In chapter 20, Mary Magdalene discovers the empty tomb. Jesus appears to her. Although she had first thought Jesus to be the gardener, she recognizes her Teacher. Jesus appears to the disciples and even convinces Thomas of his presence—Thomas who needed physical proof. Chapter 21 may be an addition. Some people have found trivial or confusing this appendage that starts with the story of the fishermen who are not doing well until Jesus comes along and instructs them to cast their nets on the right side of the boat. How could these fishermen go back to work so soon after the marvelous resurrection and appearances of their risen Lord? Well, being hard-working fishermen, of course they went back to work right away doing what they did best: fishing. This insight came to me from a sermon, "Easter's Over, I'm Going Fishing," preached by Edmon L. Rowell Jr. and recorded in his book *Finding God in the Rest of the Story*.[10] Having grown up in Rockport, Massachusetts, I realized that John and Edmon Rowell understand the psychology of fishermen.

Like fishermen anywhere, these biblical fishermen stop for breakfast and share bread and fish. Jesus asks Peter three times if Peter loves him. Peter affirms his love three times. I have heard sermons over the years that proclaim this threefold declaration of love as evidence that even though Peter had denied Jesus three times, Peter and Jesus were reconciled.

Jesus, the Good Shepherd, tells Peter to feed his lambs (21:15). The right and proper ethical response is to love God and neighbor. Peter is called to be a shepherd like Jesus. Good shepherds make good pastors, and good pastors make good churches. The redactor had ecclesiastical concerns in mind that will continue in the rest of the story of John's community that is told in the Letters of John.

---

10. Rowell, *Finding God*, 31–32.

Part Two: The Community of the Word

The World in Front of the Text
Art Activity

Art from the past, and my art, are part of the foreground. Light shining in the darkness that the darkness cannot put out shines through the painting *The Nativity* (1530) by Correggio (Antoni Allegri). This painting may be found in *The Art Book*, published by Phaidon Press. The Christ child held in Mary's loving arms is the light source that illuminates the painting. As the commentary in *The Art Book* points out, the light is so bright that a woman who looks directly at Jesus has to shield her eyes.[11] Soft light in the background conveys the dawn of a new day.

The painting *Christ before the High Priest*, by Gerrit van Honthorst, depicts the high priest questioning Jesus. This painting may be found in *Sister Wendy's 1000 Masterpieces*.[12] The high priest asserts his authority. Feeling the peace that comes from surrender to God's will, Jesus experiences God's grace, symbolized by a glow in Christ's face. Although the high priest interrogates Jesus, all the Gospels agree that the Roman prefect Pontius Pilate ordered the execution of Jesus.[13]

My watercolor image *True Vine* is based on the true vine in John chapter 15, which is so communal that I incorporated my signature into the branches in order to show solidarity with community. The true vine, which symbolizes Christ, nourishes the branches. Christ nourishes Christians in community so that they may grow, bear fruit and experience abundant and eternal life in the present.

In prayer, Jesus says that he glorified God on earth by finishing the work that God wanted him to do. In my watercolor painting *Jesus's Prayer,* (page 80) the swirling circle symbolizes God's glory. With one foot off the ground, Jesus is about to leave this earth and ascend to God the Father.

I offer a thought for your consideration: In our world in front of the text, it is important to consider how to understand New Testament texts in the friendliest way possible. As we have seen, the Christian movement was the only way for the community of the beloved disciple to proceed on their collective journey towards God. So what do bridge-building Christians do when other Christians, quoting John 14:6 ("Jesus said, 'I am the way, the truth, and the life. No one comes to the Father except through me.'") insist that the only way to God is through Jesus?

---

11. Phaidon, *Art Book*, 109.
12. Beckett, *Sister Wendy's 1000 Masterpieces*, 214.
13. *Harper's Bible Commentary*, 1005.

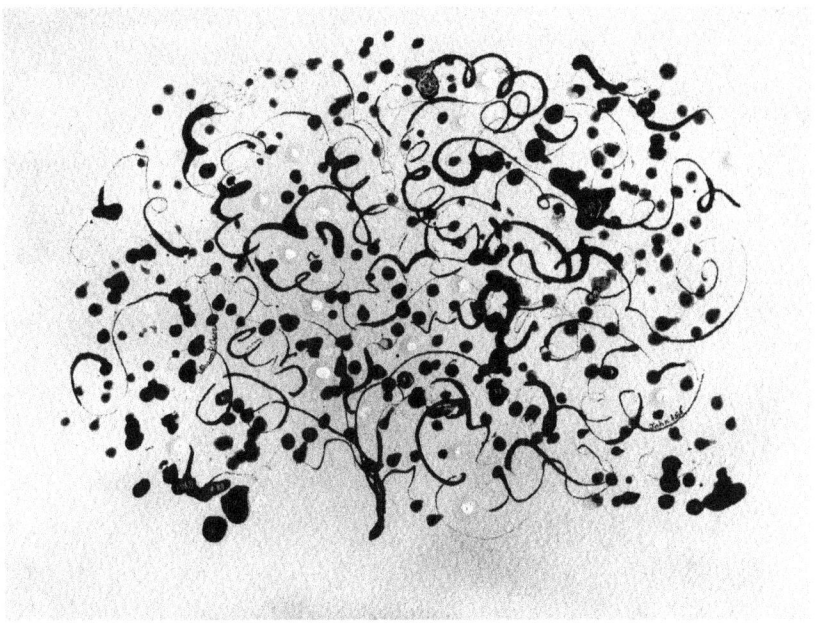

True Vine, Sharon R. Chace

My suggestion is to consider John 14:6 as an expression of Christian mysticism or of the union of the individual with Christ. In many ways, John was written to introverted insiders who did not feel at home in the world. Their emotional style and situation certainly could invite openness to seeing any signs of indwelling, divine love that is the gift of the Holy Spirit or closeness to Jesus. When shared by others in community, this union of Christ with believers is a bond of industrial-strength glue, or a kind of social mysticism. My thesis is that when readers study John with the Old Testament book Song of Solomon in mind, they will notice the intimate nature of John's claims. Jesus was life for John's community and then, as now, must have also fed individual souls. Read as mysticism, the Fourth Gospel invites individuals closer to Christ through belief and prayer, social awareness, and service. Both the people of John's community and twenty-first-century Christians have mystical dimensions in their traditions that invite mystical interpretation of John. The Song of Solomon, originally a love story between a man and a woman, may have been understood allegorically even before the Hebrew canon was stabilized in 90 AD.[14] Similarly, Christians have for centuries read the Song of Solomon as an allegory of the

---

14. Pelikan, *Jesus through the Centuries*, 125.

Jesus's Prayer, Sharon R. Chace

mystical bond between Christ and the church. The monastic tradition has viewed it as an allegory of Christ and the individual soul.

In mysticism, which is heightened religious experience, there are typically three stages of the ascent to God. These rungs are purification, illumination, and union. The ascent there and these three stages are all present in John. The first stage of ascent theme is fairly explicit in John 1:51, with the suggestion that Jesus is like Jacob's ladder: "And he said to him, 'Very truly, I tell you, you will see heaven opened and the angels of God ascending and descending upon the Son of Man.'"

Purification, the second stage of ascent to God, is an implicit concern in John's Gospel. In the first verse of chapter 2, Jesus fills jars—not just any old containers, but jars that were used in the Jewish rite of purification—with water that turned into wedding wine. Early in his ministry (an incident recorded in chapter 2), an angry Jesus cleanses the Temple. Then in 3:25, a discussion arises that highlights the purifying aspects of baptism. Next, John the Baptist insists that he is not the bridegroom (whom the readers understand as Jesus) but the friend of the bridegroom. The implication is that bridegroom was to witness to the purity of marriage. There may be veiled allusions to the Old Testament book Hosea, which features an unfaithful wife.

The third stage of illumination is clearly evident in the story of the Samaritan woman, who clearly recognizes Jesus as the Messiah or Christ (4:25). Whether this story is precise history or history beneath the surface of faithful fiction, it reflects the time-honored experiences of Jesus's followers across the centuries. In chapter 9, the unfolding of the blind man's sight that results in seeing and believing is a high point of illumination.

There are allusions to mystical union in three passages: "Those who eat my flesh and drink my blood abide in me, and I in them" (6:56); "Abide in me as I abide in you" (15:4); and "If you keep my commandments, you will abide in my love, just as I have kept my Father's commandments and abide in his love" (15:10). Mystical overtones affirm Christ's loyal commitment and abiding love for each and every soul. In personal, mystical moments of communion, Christ is the one-and-only.

9

The Letters of First, Second, and Third John
First John: God is Light, Righteousness, and Love

Background
What Kind of Work Is 1 John? When and Where Was It Written?

FIRST JOHN is an encouraging, poetic essay that was most likely written in Ephesus around 100 AD. Martin Luther said that it could buoy up afflicted hearts.[1] John Wesley found it to be a full and deep compendium of genuine Christianity.[2] The author was not likely the same author as the Gospel of John. Yet we will call the author John in regard to tradition. All three letters of John are often attributed to one author. As a leader in his community, John wanted faithful, loyal people to carry on traditional beliefs and practices. Listeners were early Christians who needed to remember that Jesus was a historical person.

Why Was 1 John Written?

John states his purpose in 5:13: "I write these things to you who believe in the name of the Son of God, so that you may know that you have eternal life." The second chapter suggests that the author wrote to warn people about other people who had left the community because of different beliefs. Some scholars think those who left the Johannine community were Docetists or had docetic inclinations. Duling and Perrin discuss the second letter of John as continuing the argument against Docetism.[3] Some things are a matter of degree, and so it is with heresy, which is an idea contrary to the accepted beliefs of a religious community. The introductory notes in the *HarperCollins Study Bible* state that most scholars suggest

---

1. *New Interpreter's Bible*, 12: 378.
2. Ibid., 365.
3. Duling and Perrin, *New Testament: Proclamation and Parenesis, Myth and History*, 441.

that the people who departed from traditional beliefs were in some way connected with Docetism, a belief that Jesus the Christ was a spirit rather than a physical human being. The opponents of John's community may have not thought that Jesus was to be identified with the divine Christ or that his death did not have value for salvation.[4] In a similar vein, yet with a slightly lesser degree of certainty about the term *Docetic*, Raymond E. Brown says that "there is no reason to think that they were docetists who denied the reality of Jesus's humanity; rather the religious import of that humanity is at issue."[5] An example, in his view, is that the opponents seem to have neglected the bloody death of Jesus as an act of love. Words to the opponents are in (1:7; 2:2; 4:10; 5:6). Whether those opposing the teachings of John's community were full-blown Docetist or had Docetic tendencies, the Gospel of John emphasizes the contrasts of good and evil and the opposition of the world. Therefore, it would be easy for some people in John's ongoing community to conclude that being human is not all that important. By denying the full humanity of Christ, people with that point of view robbed themselves of the consolation of knowing that Jesus shared our lot and understands the human condition. Despite the spiritual contrasts of dark and light, and distrust of the wider world, John's picture of Jesus makes it clear that Jesus was a real person.

Contrasting the Gospel of John with 1 John shows different concepts of the word. "The Prologue of I John does not emphasize the incarnation of the personified Word, as does the Prologue of John; rather, it testifies to the *word (message) of life* which was seen, heard, and felt—the human career of Jesus."[6] Put more succinctly in the Gospel of John, Jesus is the incarnate word. In 1 John, "word" or "word of life" is the Christian life-giving proclamation about Jesus.

The most striking, artistic feature of 1 John is curvy line. The author writes in a circular manner and returns to different ways of saying God is love. This text of God's love is life giving to faithful people of many churches over many centuries.

---

4. Rensburger, "Introduction," 2293.
5. Brown, *Introduction to the New Testament*, 390.
6. Ibid., 389.

The Text

Prologue (1:1–4)

Fellowship comes from belief in the divine life made visible in Jesus. Faith gives believers fellowship with one another. Basic proclamation is that eternal life was made manifest in the Son.

Part One: God Is Light (1:5–3:10)

God is light. Walking according to the light is righteousness. If we walk in light we have fellowship. If anyone sins, he or she has an advocate, Jesus Christ (2:1–2). We know God if we obey his commandments. Whoever hates another walks in darkness. Do not love the world (2:15). (At this point, John sees the world as a symbol of inordinate desire for pleasures and worldly wealth.) The world is passing away (2:17). The implication is that the church is leaning into the future: "See what love the Father has given us, that we should be called children of God" (3:1). We are children of God now. What we will be has not yet been exactly revealed but we will be like him. Everyone who does what is right is righteous.

Part Two: Love One Another (3:11–4:6)

"You have heard from the beginning that we should love one another" (3:11). "Whoever does not love abides in death" (3:14). John asks how God's love could abide in anyone who sees brother or sister in need and refuses help: "Little children, let us love, not in word or speech, but in truth and action" (3:18). Jesus has come in the flesh from God (4:2). The moral thrust of this assertion is that those who abide in God love one another. Loving one another flows for one's relationship with a loving God.

Part Three: God Is Love (4:7–5:12)

> Beloved, let us love one another, because love is from God; everyone who loves is born of God and knows God . . . God is love, and those who abide in love abide in God, and God abides in them . . . There is no fear in love, but perfect love casts out fear . . . We love because he first loved us. Those who say, "I love God," and hate their brothers or sisters, are liars . . . The commandment we have from him is this: those who love God must love their brothers and sisters also. (4:7–5:12)

Epilogue

The basic proclamation in 1 John 5:6–12 is that Jesus Christ is the Son of God and the way to life. Acceptance of him is the way to life. The author stresses that he is writing so that those who believe in the name of Jesus know that they have eternal life. He concludes with one last warning about idols.

The World in Front of the Text

God's Geometry

A derivative concept that I call "God's geometry" has stood up over time. The only math I really loved was geometry in my sophomore year of high school in 1959–1960. I wondered, as have other young people over the years, if the existence of God could be proved through geometric reasoning. No, apparently not. However, the next summer at church camp, our teachers, who were Congregational ministers and seminary students, gave us campers a diagram in the form of a triangle. God was named at one point of the triangle, other people at another point, and you or oneself at the remaining point on the triangle. The idea is that the three-pointed triangle is a symbol of relationships and the flow of love. So even if geometry could not prove that God exists, a geometric shape could describe a right relationship to God, to one another, and to our individual selves. In college, I brought up this concept, to the delight of my Methodist professors. This diagram has staying power. There is a more detailed version called "The Circuit of Love in 1 John" in the *New Interpreter's Bible*.[7] It is my hope that even when the details of the background of the Letters of John or the nature of the church disputes in John's community fade in importance, you will still recall God's love triangle. Unlike human triangles that generally describe a competitive romantic relationship, God's geometry keeps divine love in circulation.

Activity: Art Project

When I was in the third grade, the girls in our church group embroidered "God Is Love" in cross-stitch. The fabric was natural muslin about eight by eight inches square. We used red embroidery floss with two strands. The adult leader (C. 1953) drew the cross-stitch design in pencil on a square of unbleached muslin and made a fringe on the outside edge of the square. Today arts-and-crafts stores carry indelible markers and waterproof paint

---

7. *New Interpreter's Bible*, 12:436.

pens to use in drawing the cross-stitch design onto the fabric. I found that fourth-grade girls liked to do this project in split-stitch as well as cross-stitch. You could draw the words "God Is Love" and stitch the words with split-stitch. Using two strands of embroidery floss or crewel yarn, make one stitch and come up through the middle of the stitch and make another. Keep going. Boys might prefer wood burning.

Second John: Love One Another
Background
What Kind of Work Is 2 John?

When and where was it written? Second John is a letter with a black-and-white approach to conflict. This letter, written around 100 AD, probably in Ephesus, continues the theme of loving one another.

Who Wrote 2 John, and Why Was It Written?

The author is an anonymous elder who had spiritual and moral authority. Quite possibly, he was a beloved worship leader with preaching skills to argue against Docetism. This letter was written to the "elect lady," who was a symbol for a congregation. The "elect lady" might be an individual or a symbol of Christian community. In any case, she could be a metaphor for a protective mother who wants to bar intruders from tearing her family apart. These intruders are people who deceive others by not taking seriously Jesus's humanity. The author's perspective is that loving one another is a form of protection. The letter was written to help people through church conflict and stresses love yet at the same time calls on readers to refuse hospitality to their opponents.

The Text

The congregation is greeted with wishes of grace, mercy, and peace from Jesus Christ (1:3). Following the greeting, there are points of instruction. The author reminds his readers of the commandment to love one another. Love means walking according to the commandments (v. 5). He warns the congregation about people who do not believe that Jesus was a real man who lived on earth. Love one another, but do not be too nice to those outside the community (1:10–11).

The World in Front of the Text

Is there ever protection in avoiding people who see religion and morality very differently than do people in your faith community or your family?

Third John: Greet Friends and Imitate What Is Good

Background

Third John is a letter that was likely written around 100 AD in Ephesus. By this time, individual churches were units of the wider church. This third letter from an elder is written to Gaius. It is like a letter of recommendation and praises Gaius for his hospitality. Another description is a verbal group portrait of a divided church. This letter is also a sociological glimpse at the place of hospitality in John's community. "The elder" who wrote this letter is probably the same person who wrote 2 John. He encourages people to love one another and to guard against theology that goes against tradition. The author sees through the criteria of imitation of good. His perspective is affected by fear of doctrinal contamination. Goodness comes from God.

The Text

Hospitality to missionaries is a good thing, assuming they represent the teachings of John's community. The author is happy that people are walking in truth and supporting church workers. Gaius is praised for being hospitable. Such hospitality empowers people to be co-workers with the truth. Perhaps the most significant verse in this whole short book is, "Beloved, do not imitate what is evil but imitate what is good. Whoever does good is from God; whoever does evil has not seen God" (v. 11).

The World in Front of the Text

Something To Consider

Is hospitality related to welcome and acceptance? Is your faith community welcoming and accepting? Why or why not?

Art Activity

Draw, paint, or sculpt from any modeling compound a symbol of hospitality, such as a wreath or a pineapple. Symbols of faith, which do suggest defining beliefs of your faith community, could be placed on the wreath.

Part Three

Theological Problem and Introduction to Pauline Thought

10

Introducing Paul

THIS INTRODUCTION to Paul is largely based on the chapter "General Issues in Paul's Life and Thought" in the book *An Introduction to the New Testament* by Raymond E. Brown.[1] There are two biblical sources for information about Paul, who during his lifetime was not known as St. Paul. These sources are the body of Paul's letters and the book of Acts. Some scholars trust Acts as completely factual, and others dismiss any contention that the book is a precisely accurate historical document. Brown took a middle position by using Paul's letters as the most important sources and by cautiously using Acts for supplementary details.

Paul was born between 5 and 10 AD, during the reign of Emperor Augustus. He was a young man when Stephen was stoned (Acts 7:58). He is described as an old man and prisoner in verse 9 of Philemon, which was written after 55 AD. Paul had two names. Saul was his Jewish name. Paul was his name as a Roman citizen.

Probably, Paul was born in Tarsus and educated there. He studied with the esteemed Gamaliel, a famous Jewish rabbi of the time. Paul wrote in Greek and quoted from the Jewish Scriptures in the Greek version. He studied speech writing in the Hellenistic or Greek tradition. Paul also learned tent making, a trade he later used to support himself so he would not be a burden to faith communities. Tarsus was a city where Paul could learn about Gentiles, pagans, and philosophers such as the Stoics.

Saul persecuted the church with zeal (Acts 8:1–9; Gal 1:13–17). Then he had a life-changing experience and revelation. On the road to Damascus, Saul experienced a blinding light and heard a voice saying, "Saul, Saul, why do you persecute me?" (Acts 9:4). He understood the voice as the call of Jesus. Paul knew that his encounter with the risen Lord Jesus meant that the crucifixion and the scandal of the cross were not the end of Jesus' story. People in many church traditions consider the shift in names from Saul to Paul as symbolism of Paul's change of heart about

---

1. Brown, *Introduction to the New Testament*, 422–45.

Jesus and about the emerging Christian way. Scholars may or may not agree, but the symbolism of a name change as marking a turning point feels so right in the hearts of many.

For Paul, the story of the risen Christ continued. God renewed his call and covenant with Israel through the ministry, crucifixion, and resurrection of Jesus. Paul valued the Israelite law but found that it did not sufficiently meet his religious need to maintain a relationship with God. Justification by faith was his core belief that was honed and articulated in intellectual battles with his opponents. There are two basic aspects to justification for faith in Christ and having the faith of Christ:

1. God's graciousness in judgment has an apocalyptic or future dimension.
2. A renewed relationship between a human being and God is already effected by God's gracious action in Christ.

Paul's work differs from Matthew's. Unlike Matthew, who stressed the teachings of Jesus and the kingdom of God, Paul does not dwell on either the kingdom of God or the wise sayings of Jesus; nor does Paul accent Jesus as the true interpreter of the law as does Matthew. Paul stresses the death and resurrection of Christ. In 1 Cor 15:3–9, Paul passes on the earliest New Testament tradition about Jesus' death and resurrection. Some scholars think this is a creed passed on because Paul uses the words "delivered" and "received"—words for handing on tradition in the Judaism of his time.[2] Duling and Perrin immediately go on to say, in summary, that the big hints that Paul quoted from a source rather than making up this story are the use of words that Paul does not usually use: the plural of the Greek word for "sin," the perfect passive ("was raised"), the phrase "on the third day," and the term "the twelve" in its Greek form are all unusual terms for Paul:

> For I handed on to you as of first importance what I in turn had received; that Christ died for our sins and in accordance with the scriptures, and that he was buried, and that he was raised on the third day in accordance with the scriptures, and that he appeared to Cephas, then to the twelve. (1 Cor 15:3)

Motivated by the love of God, Paul was called to preach. He experienced difficult traveling conditions as well as hostility and anxiety about the churches, but he endured. He was true to himself, and he had to proclaim the message that no earthly power can separate us from the love of God

---

2. Duling and Perrin, *New Testament*, 163.

in Christ Jesus our Lord (Rom 8:37–39). Scholars have identified Paul's missionary activity and have constructed three missionary journeys during the periods of between 46 and 49 AD, between 50 and 52, and between 54 and 58. The basic idea is that the Christian movement spread beyond Antioch, where disciples were first called Christians (Acts 11:26).

After the first journey, there was a big meeting in Jerusalem in 49 AD (Acts 15:1–29; Gal 2:1–10). Delegates had to work out the requirements for being Christian. Paul had formed faith communities of Gentiles, with no ties to Judaism. There were many debates. The decision was made that Gentiles could become Christians without the keeping the tradition of circumcision. Food laws were not neatly settled and seem to have swung one way and then another, but these tensions worked out over time.

Around 58 to 60 AD, Paul was arrested in Jerusalem. In 60 or 61, Paul was sent to Rome on a long sea voyage, which is told in exciting detail in Acts 27:1—28:16. Paul was sent to Rome because when Festus invited King Agrippa to hear Paul's case in Caesarea, Paul appealed to Caesar, who was the head of all heads of state. Paul was a prisoner in Rome for about two years and died under Nero's rule sometime after 64 AD.

Paul's contributions to the New Testament are at least seven letters that are clearly his own. He inspired the next generation of writers in his line of thought. There are six letters attributed to Paul but written by his followers. The letters that Paul definitely wrote are 1 Thessalonians, 1 Corinthians, 2 Corinthians, Philippians, Philemon, Galatians, and Romans. A sentence that helps recall Paul's letters is: *The compassionate Christian prays, praises, gives, and remembers.*

Paul's letters are both similar to and different from letters in his culture. Paul follows the basic form of his day that includes an introduction, a central section, and a conclusion. His most important innovation is changing the customary greeting to a religious greeting that is a combination of key words from both Jewish and Greek traditions. Those words are *grace* (from the Greek tradition) and *peace* (from the Hebrew tradition). Rooted in Judaism, Paul had a mission to the Gentiles. Of course, he hoped all Judaism would follow him into emerging Christianity. That did not happen, and the Gentile reception came as something of a surprise. Paul had to deal with that development. His greeting ("Grace and peace") conveys his vision of integration and new ways of understanding God's love.

11

The First and Second Letters to the Thessalonians
Wait and Work for Jesus Christ

Background to the Letters as a Unit
Why Was the New Testament Written?

THE SHORT answer is, because Christ did not return. Therefore, it was important to write down the teachings of the earthly Jesus and to address concerns about the return of the risen Christ. Paul expected Christ to return in his lifetime. but he was premature. Diminished expectations undermine hope for individuals and communities. As a missionary and theologian, he had to explain the situation and therefore wrote 1 Thessalonians.

"Scholars are almost equally divided"[1] about whether or not Paul wrote 2 Thessalonians. Two features of 2 Thessalonians that suggest Paul did not write it include the omission of Paul's triad of faith, hope, and love and a slight advance in the importance of Jesus.[2] This increased stress on Jesus is subtly suggested by nuances in wording in 2 Thessalonians 2:16 that put Jesus first instead of God. There is a tilt towards equality: God and Jesus and Jesus and God.

While it is important to note the similarities and differences between these two New Testament letters, it is helpful to study these letters as a unit. Comparing and contrasting the different angles on the delay of Christ's return highlights the tension between Christian love and joy in the present and yearnings for the fullness of Christ's presence in the future.

The literary structure of the letters is the same, and both have a theme of apocalyptic eschatology, although they present different understandings about the Day of the Lord or of Christ's return. In 1 Thessalonians, Paul

---

1. Brown, *Introduction to the New Testament*, 591.
2. Duling and Perrin, *New Testament*, 263–64.

emphasizes the present realization of faith, hope, and love. Christian life is preparation for the imminent return of Jesus, yet Paul maintains that Christ will return by surprise, or "like a thief in the night" (5:2), so no one will know when.

In 2 Thessalonians, the author needs to stress that the Day of the Lord is not already present. Other teachers had overemphasized their closeness with Christ or perhaps had seen their suffering as the start of Christ's coming. In any case, these teachers did not place enough emphasis on the future work that God and Christ had to do to bring in the reign of God. By extending the time frame, the author of the Thessalonian letters accounted for the delay.

First Thessalonians: Lead a Life Worthy of God

Background

What kind of work is 1 Thessalonians?
When and where was it written?

First Thessalonians is a letter written in 51 or 52 AD from Corinth. This letter is the oldest book, or "earliest complete document,"[3] in the New Testament, the beginnings of Christian literature, and a classic text of Christian friendship.

Paul wrote his letter and included Silvanus and Timothy as cosenders. They wrote to the house church in Thessalonica, a port city on the northern shore of the Aegean Sea. The city was the capital of the Roman province of Macedonia, but the culture remained Greek. This is important because it explains why Paul in 1 Thess 2:3–8 presents himself as an ideal philosopher whose lifestyle proves he did not act out of greed. Some people in the Thessalonian house church were Gentile, and other members were Jewish in origin, but at least according to 2:14, Gentiles predominated. In a gesture of friendship, Paul fourteen times addresses the Thessalonians as brothers and sisters.

Paul's rhetoric, or way of talking, is similar to the way a quality-control manger might talk who is developing a training manual. Quality-control managers can be employees' friends because quality keeps a company in business. Paul was a friend who could keep the church going strong. His overall goal was to help the Thessalonians "lead a life worthy of God" (2:12). Paul, like a quality control manager who wants constant improve-

---

3. Harrington, *Who Is Jesus?* 81.

ments in quality and production, had a letter-writing strategy. He wanted improvements in decorum and independence (4:11) as well as a team effort to encourage one another and together to build the quality program (5:11). A quality-control manager of a window company, for example, will eventually have to take window samples to a testing lab to see if the frames are tight, if seals stick, and if the window can withstand hurricanes. Paul, speaking not only for himself but also on behalf of the other senders of the letter, says that they do not speak "to please mortals but to please God" (2:4). Desire to please God is a window through which to test spiritual life to see if religious community can withstand storms. As friend and quality director, Paul helped the Thessalonians build a strong faith community.

Paul wrote because he could not visit at the time. Sadness from separation is especially poignant in this letter. Paul yearns to be with his flock and is worried about the faith community that he founded. Feeling lonely, he refers to Silvanus, Timothy, and himself as "orphans" (2:17). Timothy visited the community in Thessalonica and learned that the people were strong in their faith but were anxious because Paul had not returned to visit them. Paul wrote to gently encourage the people to continue their turn from their pagan past to worship of the true God. His pastoral advice was to lead an ethical life in the present with hope for the return of Christ.

Paul evaluated quality of faith and life through the ideal of walking in holiness to prepare for the return of Jesus. His perspective was that it is mandatory to keep up loving one another (3:12) and maintaining the quality of holiness in personal life (4:1–8).

Line of the Text

First Thessalonians is a text of comfort and consolation, contrasting distinctions from the common culture and colorful themes. There is comfort in Paul's greeting when he refers to the "church . . . in God the Father and the Lord Jesus Christ" (1:1). If you were sad because people were mean to you because of your faith, and you were separated from the leaders of your church, wouldn't you find consolation in the conviction that you are in God the Father and the Lord Jesus Christ? In his warm and affectionate letter, Paul remembers the Thessalonians' "works of faith, labors of love, and steadfastness of hope" (1:3). The gospel message came to Paul's favored flock not only through the word of rational thought but through heartfelt reception of the Holy Spirit. Paul's strongest praise for anyone is for the example and faithfulness of the Thessalonians, who in spite of persecutions, received the gospel with joy (1:6–7). Their acceptance of the gospel had become famous all over Greece. Paul acknowledges their turn from pagan worship to worship of the true God. Paul had both maternal and paternal feelings for his flock. He mentions that he and Timothy and Silvanus had treated the Thessalonians gently, as a nurse would, and had also encouraged them, as a father would (2:7–12). In Paul's day, nurses played a part in the maturation of children. Paul's nurturing bent must have been comforting.

Paul acknowledges the Thessalonians' suffering from "compatriots," or other Gentiles, and persecution that is as intense as former persecution from some Jews. Sharpness arouses suspicions that someone is upping the ante beyond Paul. In chapter 2, verses 14–16 may be a latter addition or may reflect a very specific situation.[4] In any case, challenging opposition from "compatriots," or contemporaries who did not become Christians, must have brought the Thessalonians closer together in bonds of support and prayer.

The early church contrasted sharply with the prevailing culture. Changing from pagan culture to belief in the one God of Israel (who was also the Father of Jesus the Christ) was a huge change in understanding the heart of the universe. So, naturally, the Thessalonians were known for their beliefs and prone to persecution. Many Thessalonians must have lost friends because following Christ meant that they could no longer belong to pagan organizations that were like clubs. Paul was concerned for his flock and sent Timothy to check up on them. Timothy reported encouraging news of the faith, hope, and love.

Holiness and walking with God are colorful themes in 1 Thessalonians—themes that are distinctive contrasts with the common Greek culture. Motivated by a desire to please God, Paul advised leading an ethical life worthy of God. Marriage is portrayed in rather confusing verses as holy and sacred (4:1–14). Paul calls the Thessalonians, who are his glory and joy, to standards of personal holiness that command the respect of others. Distinctive holiness served the good of community and served as a missionary example to all.

Belief in Jesus's resurrection gave assurance of his return, and of the future resurrection of the faithful. Chapter 4 verses 13–18 describe Jesus's return The Greek word translated "coming" (4:15) "was a technical term for a ruler's state visit."[5] The Greek word also connotes "presence."[6] Thus, the

---

4. Krentz, "Introduction," 2218–19.

5. *HarperCollins Study Bible*, 2223.

6. Duling and Perrin, *New Testament*, 603.

metaphor stems from political life and from the greeting of royal figures, as well as from apocalyptic expectations. Paul is convinced that Christ will come again yet at the same time says that the Lord will come like "a thief in the night," which implies surprise (5:2–4). This wish for the return of Jesus is a common early-church expectation. Whether this statement should be taken literally is a matter of debate. Yet certainly God and Jesus have things to do that people alone cannot do to bring about the reign of God. In any case, there is hope for reunion, which will be powerful and permanent.

Themes of light and darkness accent this letter. The Thessalonians were "children of the light" who lived in faith, hope, and love (5:5). Having practiced these virtues, they were equipped for the struggle and could engage with confidence in life's battles. The metaphorical "breastplate of faith and love" promised protection and strength (5:8). Life in community is made strong by encouraging the fainthearted, helping the weak, seeking to do good rather than repaying evil with evil, rejoicing, praying and giving thanks (5:14–15): "Rejoice always, pray without ceasing, give thanks in all circumstances" (5:16–18).

The World in Front of the Text

Think about faith, hope, and love both as personal protection and as safeguards of the spiritual health of faith communities.

Second Thessalonians: The Love of God and the Steadfastness of Christ Will Help You Be Steadfast

Background

What Kind of Work Is 2 Thessalonians, and Where Was It Written?

Second Thessalonians is a letter with emphasis on the distant Day of the Lord as the focal point. If Paul wrote this letter, it was written about 51 or 52 AD in Corinth. If he did not write it, this letter might have been written in the late first century when people were very concerned about when the Day of the Lord would come.[7]

By Whom Was 2 Thessalonians Written?

To repeat, scholars are divided about equally over whether or not Paul wrote this letter, which is addressed to the Thessalonians. Because this

---

7. Brown, *Introduction to the New Testament*, 591.

letter corrects a view that could so easily be overdone, my sense is to assume that if Paul was not the author, the author knew Paul and his circumstances so well that Paul might as well have written most of it.

The Line of Thought in the Text Leads the Thessalonians to Keep on Working

We can imagine Paul's pastoral predicament, whether or not he wrote this letter. Paul had written a wonderful letter of Christian friendship that we know as 1 Thessalonians. He was so pleased that the Thessalonians had accepted the gospel that he did not have to even mention his favorite themes of justification by faith alone. He knew that the second coming would come by surprise, but he was so certain that it would come soon that he emphasized the present realization of faith, hope, and love. However, the Thessalonians' understanding of the present dimensions of the reign of God had gone too far. (A tendency to overinterpret pastoral meditations in church newsletters is sometimes an ongoing problem.) So now Paul, or the author, had to state very clearly that the Day of the Lord was not already here (2:3). In Paul's thought, people who had not obeyed the gospel would be separated from the presence of God (1:9). (Separation from God, whether in this life or after death, is one abstract definition of hell.) The mystery of evil activity was already at work, although lawlessness would be no match for God's ultimate power. The exhortation or preaching was to hold fast to tradition and know that through grace there is eternal comfort and good hope (2:15–17). The Thessalonians were getting carried away with expectations for Jesus's return. We can imagine them wondering why they should work if the end is near. The main point in 2 Thessalonians is keep away from those who live in idleness for whatever reasons. Paul gently tells the idlers to work (3:6–14). If he had known the present-day hymn, "Work, For the Night Is Coming," this hymn would be the pick of the day.

The World in Front of the Text

The late children's television pioneer Mr. Rogers was a Presbyterian minister. When young children are troubled by evil, Mr. Rogers advised, parents should tell young children to look to the helpers. He also told parents to say that they will do all they can to protect their children. When you see evil in the world, what helps you remain steadfast in your faith?

12

The Letter to the Ephesians
Alive Together in Christ, the Church is Knitted Together by Love

Editorial Preface and Contrasting Picture of Church Life

There are two features of Ephesians that I most want readers to remember:

1. The compiler of this letter introduces and expands Paul's thought.
2. The author of Ephesians paints a different picture of the church than is found in the letters that were definitely written by Paul.

Background
A Reflective Letter

Ephesians is a reflective letter by an author who wrote in Paul's spirit. Because the letter is written to people in general rather than to a specific church or individual, the letter sounds like an essay for a wide audience. Edgar J. Goodspeed saw this writing as an introduction to Paul's letters and the letters written in Paul's name.[1] In writing his introduction, the author probably drew upon the letters Paul definitely wrote, and upon Colossians. This letter-essay is a standard kind of Pauline communication that is in keeping with Paul's thought yet written for a new time and place. In contrast to Paul's First Letter to the Corinthians, which contains verbal, close-up snapshots of the local community, Ephesians is like a panoramic photograph of the wider or universal church, taken with a wide-angle lens. This letter-essay was written in about AD 90 to all the saints in Ephesus

---

1. Goodspeed, *Introduction to the New Testament*, 222.

who were faithful. Where was this letter-essay written? Ephesus may be the place of writing.

A Letter By an Excellent Compiler and Editor

An admirer who was an excellent disciple of Paul wrote Ephesians. Three characteristics that suggest the writing does not come from Paul are much longer sentences, a general audience, and new developments in the understanding of church. The long sentences are in Greek. Examples of the long Greek sentences are found in chapter 1 in verses 15 through 23 (9 verses), in chapter 3 in verses 1 through 7 (7 verses), and in chapter 4, in verses 11 through 16 (6 verses).[2] English translations break them into shorter sentences. Unlike letters definitely written by Paul, this letter does not include a cosender, nor does it address a specific problem or historical situation. In Ephesians the emphasis is on the universal church rather than a local church.

Only a very few scholars think Paul himself wrote this letter. According to Raymond. E. Brown, 70 to 80 percent of critical scholars reject the view that Paul wrote this letter.[3] My college professor of New Testament, John L. Cheek, liked to tell us that his divinity school professor Edgar J. Goodspeed mentioned the possibility that Onesimus of Ephesus, the runaway slave who was nurtured by Paul, might have written this letter. In a similar vein, Raymond E. Brown discusses in his words Goodspeed's "adventurous explanation." In summary, Onesimus was released by Philemon (from slavery) and went on to become the bishop of Ephesus and composer of Ephesians as a summary of collected letters of Paul.[4] Goodspeed did not claim certainty. However, even the chance that Onesimus collected Paul's writings warms the hearts of even the most reserved scholars who prefer understatement.

In any case, the author wanted to summarize Pauline thought. Even though Paul did not likely write Ephesians, in some ways he might as well have, because the author had exceptional editorial skills and indirectly quoted many of Paul's favorite themes and words. Some of these themes are salvation by faith through grace (2:8), the new self as new creation (4:24), and living in light (5:8). Therefore, I will often refer to the author as Paul.

He reminded Christians of the great values in their faith. Paul distills his hopes for his followers into poetic prayer. After praying for inner

---

2. Duling and Perrin, *New Testament*, 274.
3. Brown, *Introduction to the New Testament*, 629.
4. Ibid., 630.

strength and for the presence of Christ in hearts, after praying that people remain rooted and grounded in love, the author offers a prayer of petition: "I pray that you may have the power to comprehend, with all the saints, what is the breadth and length and height and depth, and to know the love of Christ that surpasses knowledge, so that you may be filled with all the fullness of God" (3:18–19). The author wants people to understand that the church was meant to be in God's plan and to believe that the mystery of Christ is the unity of Jews and Gentiles in the body of Christ. Exaltation with the risen Christ is key to the understanding of salvation in Ephesians.

Artistic Description

Perspective

The author's perspective is that the universal church is founded on the apostles and that "the mystery of Christ" (3:14) means the union of Jews and Gentiles in the one body. Before Christ, Gentiles had not experienced being part of God's family, and thus they were alienated from the one God that the Israelites knew and loved. Through Christ, both Gentiles and Jews have access to God (2:18). This does not mean that Jews have to adopt Christianity to be near God, because they were already close to God. Equal access does mean that God adopted non-Jews, who were far away at the time, into the family. The inclusion of Gentiles means that Gentiles have become fellow heirs (3:6).

Business language expresses the author's perspective. The editor-author's perspective is that the church was destined by God's grace to grow from the cottage industry of 1 Corinthians into a major worldwide corporation—in the words of the New English Bible, "believers incorporate in Christ Jesus" (1:1). Christ is the head or Chief Executive Officer. As Chief Executive Officer, Christ gave spiritual gifts to use in the building up of the institution. People were bonded and knit together in a team effort (4:9–16).

Christians in this letter are Christ's partners in service and sometimes in suffering. Associates of Christ should not relapse into vice. Good people are needed to spread the word. The author of Ephesians had public relationship skills that the church needed in order to spread the message of universal and equal access to God.

Color Word: The Word Love Colors the Writing.

In chapter 3, the author's prayer is that the Ephesians will be "rooted and grounded in love" (v. 17). In chapter 4, the author writes that we should "bear . . . with one another in love" (v. 2) and "speak . . . the truth in love" (v. 15). In chapter 5, he says to "live in love" (v. 2) and that "he who loves his wife loves himself" (v. 28). Paul closes his letter with these words: "Grace be with all who have an undying love for our Lord Jesus Christ" (6:24). In Ephesians, a unique word for Jesus that is related to love is "Beloved."[5]

Metaphors for Church

In Eph 1:22–23, the church is the body of Christ with Christ as the head. The body of Christ with Christ as the head also describes the church in 4:15. In Ephesians 2:20–21, the church people or "citizens with the saints" are a household of God that grows into a holy temple. As the church grows, it is held together in Christ. In chapter 5, verses 25–27, the church is compared to the purity of a bride. Like a bride, the church deserves love.

Plot Line

The only plot or story line to give action to this thoughtful letter is found in the closing lines of personal matters and benediction. Tychicus will tell the recipients of the letter everything.

Ephesians as Editorial Introduction

The author quotes from Paul's letters and letters written in his name and spirit. Sometimes he alters the ideas slightly as if he is drawing out the implications of Paul's thought. His theological and editing skills are a gift to Paul and the developing church. Sometimes he leaves out emphases that have faded in importance, and at other times rounds out Paul's ideas. He leaves out explicit references to the Day of Judgment. The watchwords "keeping alert" extend to the indefinite future. While Paul worked at finding the synthesis of Jews and Gentiles by using a metaphor of Gentiles being grafted onto God's family tree, the author of Ephesians assumes this synthesis and develops it. The exalted Christ is stressed more than the death of Christ. Christ appoints the apostles and prophets (4:11). Whereas in letters definitely written by Paul, the church body is a loosely organized group of different people with various gifts, in Ephesians the gifts are more like institutional job descriptions assigned by Christ. Thus, Christ

---

5. *HarperCollins Study Bible*, 2194.

as head of the church is a development that goes beyond Paul. Ephesians quotes and develops large portions of Colossians. Some of the themes that the author of Ephesians appropriates from Colossians are vices, virtues, gratitude in the human heart, and the household code as reflection of the relationship between Christ and the church. Ephesians 5:3–8 reflects Colossians 3:5–8 on vices. Standard vices include sexual impurity, greed, and vulgar talk. Speaking about virtues in community, Ephesians 4:1–2 echoes Colossians 3:12–13. Gratitude is a shared concern in Eph 5:19–20 and Col 3:16–17. Common virtues are humility, gentleness, patience, and efforts to maintain unity. Household codes are metaphors in Ephesians 5:21—6:9 and Colossians 3:18—4:5.

The language of the universality of sin in Ephesians 2:1–2 is reflective of Paul, especially in Romans 3:9–18: "Alive together with Christ" (Eph 2:5) and "clothe yourselves with the new self" (Eph 4:24) are very much like "a new creation is everything," as in Galatians 6:15.

Access to God in one Spirit (2:18) reflects Paul in Romans 5:1–2 and Galatians 3:28—4:7). All Christians have access to God in the Spirit. Access for one group does not mean exclusion for another. The hymn of praise from Col 1:15–23 is reflected in Ephesians 2:14–18 through depiction of the new, cosmic unity of Jews and Gentiles.

As an author and editor, the author of Ephesians interprets Paul's military images. The author of Ephesians slightly changes Paul's metaphors of armor. In 1 Thessalonians Paul says that since we belong to the day (which is to say we live ethically in the present), people should put on the breastplate of faith and love, and a helmet—the hope of salvation (5:8). The triad of faith, hope, and love is thoroughly Pauline. In Ephesians, these images suggest slightly different spiritual dimensions. The author writes of the belt of truth (6:14), the breastplate of righteousness, and the helmet of salvation. Salvation is somewhat more completely assured through military metaphors in Ephesians. Righteousness is a direct outgrowth of faith and love. Truth also contributes to living rightly with unity in community, which is a main concern in Ephesians. In Ephesians, the outcome of salvation that "made us alive together with Christ" is being raised up or elevated in the heavenly or transcendent places with Christ (2:5–7). Unity is through the mystery of the body of Christ that is knit together in love (4:16). These intimations of cosmic unity and of salvation as elevation are present in embryonic form in 1 Thessalonians and Romans. Writing his first letter, Paul said that we are destined for obtaining salvation through our Lord Jesus Christ, who died so that we may live with him. Therefore Paul says that we are to encourage and build up one another (1 Thess 5:11).

Glorification with Christ (Rom 8:17) hints at glorification beyond earthly life. In Ephesians Paul's editor built upon Paul's theology of glorification.

Most important, Eph 2:8–10 rounds out Paul's faith-and-works contrast. Good works follow faith because people are created for good works; or put another way, people flourish when they do good deeds. Ephesians highlights the image of "the fruit of the light" that is found in the good and true, flowing from living in the light. (Eph 5:8–9). The metaphor "fruit of the light" is a variation of Paul in Gal 5:22–23, where he writes about the "fruit of the Spirit." The author of Ephesians substituted the word "saved" (2:8) for Paul's word *justified*, as, for example, in Gal 2:16. Either "justified" or "saved "is a positive way of being in God's presence.

The Line of the Text

Following the introduction, the letter unfolds as the author uses Paul's themes. After extending formal blessings, Paul responds with blessings to God: Bless God who has blessed us and adopted us as his children. We are blessed in Christ with every spiritual blessing and destined for adoption. Christ, the Beloved bestows grace (1:3–5). Reasons for blessing God include redemption and forgiveness (1:7). Paul's prayer is that the eyes of our hearts be enlightened or that what we today might call "inner vision" will enable us to know what is the hope to which we are called. A statement of faith that follows is that God is beyond all earthly rulers and destructive forces or powers, such as imperial rule in New Testament times (1:22–23). The church is the body of Christ, and Christ is the head of the universal church. Fullness suggests that the worldwide church is more than the local church.

Saved by Faith

We are saved by faith, not works, yet we are "created in Christ Jesus for good works" (2:8–10). Good works are "to be our way of life" (2:10). We are one in Christ. If the writer of Ephesians had had the hymnbooks of our day, he might have asked us to sing the hymn "In Christ There Is No East or West," or "We Are One in the Spirit."

Paul's Call

Paul's commissioned ministry brought news of the boundless riches of Christ and the wisdom of God to the Gentiles (3:7–10). Paul, as a servant of God, understood his mission to them to be part of God's plan.

Turning from emphasis on ideas to an emphasis on the ways we live, the author prays, guided by the Holy Spirit, that Christ will dwell in our hearts through faith as we are "rooted and grounded in love" (3:16–17). He wants us to comprehend the breadth, length, height, and depth and to know the love of Christ that is more than intellectual knowledge (3:14–21). Such awareness is experience of the fullness of God.

The author of Ephesians begs us to lead lives worthy of our callings, bearing with one another in love and working to maintain the unity of the Spirit. One body, one Spirit, one hope, one Lord, one baptism and one God who is above, through and in all is a unifying understanding (4:1–7). There are different jobs in the church, but a common task is to build up the church together (4:7–16). In the situation reflected in this letter, different gifts unify the church instead of dividing it, as they did in 1 Cor 12:1–31. Unity is a theme woven throughout Ephesians, and ties the letter together.

New Life in Christ

The Ephesians must turn away from their former lax standards (4:17). New life in Christ means avoiding hateful speech and not being greedy, because greed means we make things into idols or find them more important than God (5:3–5). In brief, theologian Paul Tillich defined idolatry as making things other than God our "ultimate concern."[6]

Ethics Call for Discernment

"Try to find out what is pleasing to the Lord" (5:10). Verses 19 and 20 of Ephesians 5 give us a window on early Christian prayer: "as you sing psalms and hymns and spiritual songs among yourselves, singing and making melody to the Lord in your hearts, giving thanks to God the Father at all times and for everything in the name of our Lord Jesus Christ."

The household code (5:21–33) extends the author's reflection on the church with Christ as head or source. The household code has a touch of mutuality or equality in marriage: "Be subject to one another out of reverence for Christ" (5:21). The love of the husband has more weight than wifely submission, a good feature to note in our age. Our understandings of marriage change. However, marriage in many cultures and times can reflect God's grace or Christ's sacramental love for the church. Husbands are to love their wives. The respect that a woman is urged to show her husband has a connotation of gratitude. Slavery is also accepted as a reality

---

6. Tillich, *Dynamics of Faith*, 12.

in the household code. However, slaves were educated and had far better lives than did the slaves in American history.

The World in Front of the Text

1. Consider the spiritual style in Ephesians. Compared to the many other ways of being religious in the New Testament, the spiritual style in Ephesians is especially full bodied. In the New Testament there are many ways to be religious, yet these differences are not necessarily incompatible. Different emphases address differing situations and contexts. The Gospel of Mark emphasizes the necessity of carrying the cross, accepting suffering and even martyrdom. Luke shifts the emphasis to everyday sacrificial living and imitating Jesus. Matthew teaches his followers to trust and obey Jesus as fulfillment of the Torah. The Gospel of John offers community and individuals experiences of mystical union. Paul gives assurance that by trusting in God with the faith of Jesus, and by having faith in Jesus, people are justified by faith, accepted, and worthy to be in God's presence. Ephesians's spirituality is ecumenical in application, which is very appropriate in literature that portrays the worldwide or universal church. Many kinds of Christians can find and adapt religious practices from Ephesians.

   There are three main aspects of personal and communal piety in Ephesians: a) to embrace adoption as children of God; b) to follow through on the gift of being made alive together with Christ; and c) to sing and pray with thanksgiving.

   A. Embracing adoption as children of God leads to the ethic of imitating God as beloved children and living in love as Christ lived (5:1–2). "Live as children of light—for the fruit of the light is found in all that is good and right and true. Try to find out what is pleasing to the Lord" (5:8–10). These virtues are generally helpful in building up any kind of institution. Some psychologists believe that firstborn children seek to please their parents. In similar fashion, the author of Ephesians advises the first Christians in the first stage of Christianity to find that which pleases the Lord (5:10).

   B. Following through on the gift of being made alive together with Christ leads to many kinds of peacemaking efforts. Leading a life worthy of the calling is a life of patience, of gentleness, and of making every effort possible to maintain unity and the bond of peace (4: 1–3). Speaking the truth in love helps the church work properly and grow into Christ (4:15). The author advises that church members (and, by implication, all of us) "not to let the sun go down on your anger" (4:26). From what I have experienced, going to bed angry is sometimes just part of life. My interpretation of this passage (that I have never read anywhere, but others may have thought of it) is, do not bury your anger in your inner darkness. Give your anger to God, whose sunlight is purifying.

C. Finally, singing and praying fill the heart with gratitude and strength in ancient and contemporary communities of faith. Pray in the Spirit (6:18) as the author did in embedded prayers in his introduction to Paul's writings (1:17–19; 3:14–19). Gratitude is the most ecumenical religious stance and core salute to God and life. In our culture, Thanksgiving Day is a unifying holiday that people of many faiths and of no faith community share. The author of Ephesians wrote a perfect invitation to a Methodist hymn sing focusing on thanksgiving: "Do not get drunk with wine, for that is debauchery; but be filled with the Spirit, as you sing psalms and hymns and spiritual songs among yourselves, singing and making melody to the Lord in your hearts, giving thanks to God the Father at all times and for everything in the name of our Lord Jesus Christ" (5:18–20). An ecumenical hymn sing of Christians making melody to the Lord in their hearts is a derivative image of Christian unity in love from Ephesians.

2. Contrast Ephesians 2:19–21 and 1 Corinthians 3:11. Ephesians says that the household of God is built upon prophets and apostles with Christ Jesus as the cornerstone. First Corinthians states that the church's foundation is Jesus Christ. Is this an important difference? Are churches that have bishops in charge more likely to favor the passage in Ephesians? Why or why not? Do you think that in the library of New Testament books, people have favorite books? Having favorite books is sometimes called having "the canon within the canon." What can we learn by identifying our favored books? What can we learn by reading biblical passages that challenge the way we do or see things?

3. A theme of blessing is woven like a delicate golden thread throughout Ephesians. Thanksgiving is a way of blessing God and life. Think about all that helps you bless life. People? Beauty in nature or art? Church life?

Part Four

ॐ

The Rest of Paul's Letters

13

The Letter to the Galatians

Bearing One Another's Burdens
Is Fulfilling the Law of Christ

Background

GALATIANS IS an ancient theological document and foundation of Christian freedom from the early stages of Christianity through our present day.

Freedom in Mutual Regard in the Past and in the Present

At a church coffee hour in a church that my husband served as pastor, an elderly gentleman spoke to me about his conviction that women should not have leadership positions in the church. I quoted from Galatians. "There is no longer Jew or Greek, there is no longer slave or free, there is no longer male and female; for all of you are one in Christ Jesus" (3:28). He replied, "Got me there," and then we enjoyed the coffee hour together in fellowship with our church family.

Call to Christian Freedom

Galatians is also a circulating letter and call to Christian freedom. Paul wrote this letter to the churches of Galatia around AD 54–55.[1] This letter was composed to be read aloud to each Galatian congregation and was a substitute for Paul's personal presence. The letter presents a defense of Paul's understanding of religious requirements.

---

1. Brown, *Introduction to the New Testament*, 468.

PART FOUR: THE REST OF PAUL'S LETTERS

*Freedom to Forge a New Identity in a Formative
Stage of Church Development*

In the process of forming their new faith communities, the Galatian congregations faced an identity crisis. Were they a branch of Judaism? Or were they a new community of Jewish Christians and former Gentile pagans that did not need to become Jewish before becoming Christians? Paul wanted his people to know that they could be Christians without becoming Jews first. Thus, in summary, Paul asked people to ignore the rival missionaries with their narrow view of Christianity that demanded incorporation into Judaism. In other words, according to the warring preachers, men had to be circumcised. In Paul's understanding of life in the Spirit, circumcision was not a requirement to become a Christian. In contrast to the leaders who preached a different understanding of requirements for church life, Paul preached a style of Christianity that emphasized both having faith in Christ and also having the faith and trust that Jesus had in God.

Line of Thought in the Text

Paul was not one of the original disciples, but he saw himself as an apostle. (Gal 1:1). He expresses his annoyance that some people are turning against the graced message he taught, to a different understanding (1:6–7) Paul, who had persecuted Christians, changed his mind because of revelation. He insisted that his message and calling were not from humans but from revelation (1:11–12). Paul tells us the story of his calling in Gal 1:11–24. Consider one sentence from the story of Paul's call of mission to the Gentiles: "But when God, who had set me apart before I was born and called me through his grace, was pleased to reveal his Son to me, so that I might proclaim him among the Gentiles, I did not confer with any human being" (vv. 15–16).

Paul stated that Jews and Gentiles are both offered justification. Abraham had faith in God, or "believed God and it was reckoned to him as righteousness" (Gen 15:6). This God-given justification or declaration of righteousness came before the introduction of circumcision in Genesis 17. Paul interpreted God's promise in Gen 17: 2–6 that Abraham would be the father or ancestor of all nations to mean that Abraham is the ancestor of all people, or our shared father in faith. Paul's theology of promise, in essence, is "God's promise that in Abraham all nations would be blessed—"a promise independent of circumcision—so that in giving the Spirit to the uncircumcised Gentiles, through faith, God is fulfilling the promise to Abraham, a man whose faith was reckoned as righteousness."[2] Since Abraham was made righteous through faith, faith is the most important spiritual bond among believers (3:6–9). Paul's summary is "The one who is righteous will live by faith" (3:11).

Faith has both personal and social implications. Unity in Christ is a communal bond: "There is no longer Jew or Greek, there is no longer slave or free, there is no longer male and female; for all of you are one in Christ Jesus" (3:28).

It seems to me that inclusion in God's family as children and heirs supports faith and trust that justifies and makes righteous. Paul used adoption language to explain why Gentiles can be part of God's family:

> But when the fullness of time had come, God sent his Son, born of a woman, born under the law, in order to redeem those who were under the law, so that they we might receive adoption as children. And because you are children, God has sent the Spirit of his Son into our hearts, crying, "Abba! Father!" (4:4–6)

"For in Christ Jesus neither circumcision nor uncircumcision counts for anything; the only thing that counts is faith working through love" (5:6). ("Faith working through love" is at the core of community throughout the centuries.) Paul says it is wrong to use freedom for self-indulgence (5:13), a theme that will come up again in other New Testament books. Stressing freedom from details of Jewish law, Paul summarizes the law as loving neighbor as self (5:15). Expounding upon Jesus's teachings, Paul serves Jesus by simplifying and opening up Jesus's thought that was rooted in Judaism.

If people listen to their hearts, the Spirit will inspire good living. In contrast to various forms of destructive behavior, "the fruit of the Spirit is love, joy, peace, patience, kindness, generosity, faithfulness, gentleness and self-control" (5:22–23). Paul asks his community to "bear one another's burdens and thus fulfill the law of Christ" (6:2). Sowing your seed (or putting your efforts into spiritual endeavors) will result in reaping eternal life (6:7).

Paul made a point of signing this letter in his own hand rather than having a scribe or secretary sign it for him (6:11). Cherishing the new creation, Paul closes with a personalized image of the cross, Jesus's marks in Paul's own body (6:17). In keeping with his gracious offering of life in the Spirit, Paul prays: "May the grace of our Lord Jesus Christ, be with your spirit, brothers and sisters. Amen" (6:18).

---

2. Brown, *Introduction to The New Testament*, 472.

Part Four: The Rest of Paul's Letters

The World in Front of the Text

Female readers may wonder if the emphasis on the debate about the circumcision requirement means that this letter is more for males. Eventually, baptism replaced circumcision as an identifying rite of passage. Baptism, confirmation, service, and ongoing renewal of the Spirit in communities of God's people are for both males and females. Both men and women are called to help other people bear their burdens. Believing that we are all children of God as part of a new creation means heartfelt certainty that women are as valuable as are men. Whenever hearts warm and turn, flower and bear the fruits of the Spirit, there is a personalized new creation.

What does it mean to "bear one another's burdens and thus fulfill the law of Christ"? How do you do this as an individual or as a church community?

14

The First Letter to the Corinthians
Faith, Hope, and Love Abide, and the Greatest of These is Love

Background

Letter

First Corinthians is a letter that is part of an ongoing discussion, with 2 Corinthians. The rhetorical style is deliberation or consideration of what a person or community should or should not do. Paul wrote 1 Corinthians to the Corinthians around AD 54 or 55. Most likely, he wrote from Ephesus. Sosthenes is a cosender. This congregation was mainly Gentile Christians.[1] The social conflict in (what we might metaphorically call) First Church Corinth is the background of Paul's letter.

Divided Congregation

Paul was away. He wrote to address various problems and divisions in the emerging church. The congregation quarreled over ethical issues, leadership, and what foods to eat. Each dispute provides a snapshot of local church life.

The most serious division was between rich and poor people in the house church (11:17–22). The sacrament we know as Communion or the Eucharist or the Lord's Supper was not the same for everyone. The rich, who were accustomed to elaborate Hellenistic banquets, would feast and let the poorer people come later. Paul knew that it was one thing for the rich to eat well at home with friends, but the fellowship of a communal holy meal was for the whole community. Christian love meant equal regard.

---

1. Harrington, *Who Is Jesus?* 87.

Paul maintained that Christians could eat meat sacrificed to idols because that pagan practice was meaningless. Idols are not God. But if eating sacrificial meat hurt people who still believed that idols have power, then love suggested refraining (8: 7–13). Paul's slogan was that "all things are lawful but not all things are beneficial" (6:12). Slogans were rhetorical devices that helped Paul make his points.

Some members of the congregation were very taken with the leadership of Apollos. Apollos was Paul's assistant. He was an Alexandrian Jew who knew Scripture. Paul did not blame other church leaders for their popularity, but he did insist that all church members were one in Christ.

Overcoming disunity calls for discernment. For Paul, true wisdom (as opposed to overconfident, status-linked wisdom) is found in Christ, who is wisdom from God, the source of life. Christ is the church's foundation. Different people with various gifts can all give their talents to God and the church:

> Now there are varieties of gifts, but the same Spirit; and there are varieties of services, but the same Lord; and there are varieties of activities, but it is the same God who activates all of them in everyone. To each is given the manifestation of the Spirit for the common good. (12:4–7)

Then Paul mentions a variety of gifts that all build up the body of Christ. These abilities include gifts of prophecy, teaching, healing, speaking in tongues, and various kinds of leadership.

Paul notes that the gift of speaking in tongues will not be understood except by the person speaking, unless he or she also has the gift of interpretation. Paul insists that while he could speak in tongues himself, prophecy is better because it builds up the whole church, or body of Christ. Gifts of leadership should not cause division as it did when some people thought that the gifts of speaking in tongues made them better than other people.

If Paul had not needed to stress unity, we might not have his picture of worship in the early church. Paul describes worship in the early church and the goal of building up the church. In chapter 14 Paul says that when people come together, each one has a hymn, a lesson, a revelation, a tongue, or an interpretation: "Let all things be done for building up" (14:26). In a spirit of unity, Paul urges people to give weekly to the collection for the Jerusalem church.

Artistic Elements

Perspective

Paul's perspective is that Christ crucified is foolishness to the world, but as ultimate reality Christ is the source of wisdom and power (3:18–19).

Texture

Paul writes with texture when he alludes to Old Testament passages. The most important allusion addresses common concerns about death. Writing about the resurrection in 1 Cor 15:54–55, Paul quotes Isaiah 25:7. Paul summarizes in poetry: "Death has been swallowed up in victory. Where, O death, is your victory? Where, O death, is your sting?" (15:54–55). Isaiah had written, "And he will destroy on this mountain the shroud that is cast over all peoples, the sheet that is spread over all nations; he will swallow up death forever" (Isa 25:7). Thus first-century listeners to 1 Corinthians might have said, "Our people have heard something like this before." The bottom line is trust that death no longer controls us because God has given us victory through our Lord Jesus Christ.

Focal Point

When looking at a painting, the viewer may briefly spot the focal point and then scan the entire image to look at the background and foreground. After returning to the focal point, the viewer may understand how the entire picture holds together. So it is with 1 Corinthians. Your first introduction to Paul's letter may be at a wedding when the priest or pastor reads from chapter 13, which is sometimes called the "love chapter." Christian love is the focal point of 1 Corinthians.

Line

Keeping in mind the focal point of Christian love, take a walk with Paul's line of thought in the following short summaries of each chapter. The greeting (1:4–9) contains thanksgiving for grace, acknowledgment of the Corinthians' spiritual gifts, and hopes for future blameless people.

Text

Part I: Matters That Matter as Reported by Chloe's People

Chapter 1 Because of divisions in the Corinthian church from following several church leaders, Paul urges unity in the Lord, and unity in the same mind and purpose (v. 10). He stresses that all belong to Christ rather then to Apollos or to Cephas. He stresses that while Christ crucified is a stumbling block and folly to the world; Christ—not worldly wisdom—is the power and wisdom of God. God is the source of life in Christ Jesus, who became for Paul's followers the personified wisdom from God (v. 30). To boast in the Lord is to acknowledge the source of grace.

Chapter 2 God's wisdom was revealed through the Spirit, which searches even the depths of God.

Chapter 3 Spiritual immaturity, and division resulting in jealously and quarreling are noted in 1 Cor 3:1–4. Paul planted. Apollos watered. God gave growth (3:6). By implication, church people are God's garden, as well as a building built on the one foundation of Jesus Christ, and a temple of the Holy Spirit (3:10–18). The Corinthians belong to Christ, and Christ to God (3:23). (In a society where just about everyone was practically owned by someone else, belonging to Christ was a strong statement of unity.)

Chapter 4 Do not be self-important, but, like Paul, be willing to be a fool for Christ (4:10). The role of fool or clown gave Paul a poetic and even playful way to address problems of puffiness and false pride that stemmed from wealth. Following in Jesus's way, Paul says that when reviled, we bless, and when persecuted, endure (v.12).

Chapter 5 Asserting his leadership, Paul is concerned for maintaining purity because he knows that sexual immorality is destructive in community (vv. 1–5). While the Corinthians' associating with outsiders who are immoral is unavoidable, Paul, drawing upon power in his shame-based society, is harsh on a member in his charge.

Chapter 6 Addressing a small church with strong boundaries, Paul urges his people to settle disputes among themselves rather than in secular courts (v. 1). Christian freedom does not mean disregard for the body. Paul issues his pastoral slogan: "'All things are lawful for me,' but not all things are beneficial" (6:12).

Part II. Paul Responds to Concerns of His Congregation

Chapter 7   Marriage is good, but Paul stresses the less-encumbered celibate life in light of his belief in the Lord's return. In a tone that echoes the Gospel of John, he says that the present form of the world is passing away (v. 31).

Chapter 8   Love gives perspective. Be sensitive to people's feelings about food traditions.

Chapter 9   Paul's goal is to spread the gospel without payment by being "all things to all people" (v. 22), although he states that preachers should earn their living through their work (vv. 3–4).

Chapter 10 Pagan meals are not for Christians, but food is not really an issue as long as people respect the consciences of others. Paul again states a theme song: "'All things are lawful,' but not all things are beneficial" (v. 23). Do everything to the glory of God, and try not to offend (vv. 31–32).

Chapter 11 Head coverings and long hair for women and short hair for men are the customs of the day. Nevertheless, women and men are interdependent (vv. 10–11). Reaffirming community, genuine spirituality, self-examination, and remembrance, Paul is insistent on not letting the Lord's Supper become a source of social-class divisions.

Chapter 12 There are varieties of gifts but the same Spirit. People have different spiritual gifts that are important in the body of Christ and contribute to the common good (vv. 4–7) Still "strive for . . . a more excellent way" that Paul will unpack in the next chapter.

Chapter 13 Paul praises the virtue of love. "Faith, hope, and love abide," but "the greatest of these is love" (v. 13). The focal is a hub of love that radiates like spokes in a wagon wheel throughout the whole letter and ties it together. In the New Testament there are different Greek words for "love." The New Testament Greek word for love in 1 Corinthians 13 is agape, which is

"Christian love," which is sometimes sacrificial. Other forms of love in the Bible are romantic love and friendship. In this poetic chapter, love is contrasted with other spiritual gifts and is found superior:

> If I speak in the tongues of mortals and of angels, but do not have love, I am a noisy gong or a clanging cymbal. And if I have prophetic powers, and understand all mysteries and all knowledge, and if I have all faith, so as to remove mountains, but do not have love, I am nothing. If I give away all my possessions, and if I hand over my body so that I may boast, but do not have love, I gain nothing.
>
> Love is patient; love is kind; love is not envious or boastful or arrogant or rude. It does not insist on its own way; it is not irritable or resentful; it does not rejoice in wrongdoing; but rejoices in the truth. It bears all things, believes all things, hopes all things, endures all things.
>
> Love never ends. But as for prophecies, they will come to an end; as for tongues, they will cease; as for knowledge, it will come to an end. For we know only in part, and we prophesy only in part, but when the complete comes, the partial will come to an end. When I was a child, I spoke like a child, I thought like a child, I reasoned like a child; when I became an adult, I put an end to childish ways. For now we see in a mirror, dimly, but then we will see face to face. Now I know only in part; then I will know fully, even as I have fully known. And now faith, hope, and love abide, these three; and the greatest of these is love. (13:1–13)

Chapter 14 Prophecy has more value than speaking in tongues. One who speaks in tongues should pray for an interpreter (v.13). Praying and singing with the spirit needs the counterbalance of praying and singing with the mind. Talking in tongues is witness to nonbelievers, while prophecy that may do more to build up the church is for those who already have faith. Orderly worship includes a hymn, a lesson, a revelation, a tongue, or an interpretation within restraints of time, decency, and order.

Chapter 15 "The last enemy to be destroyed is death" (v. 26). Christ's resurrection takes the sting out of death, which does not have the last word (vv. 54–55). By implication, the archenemy, sorrow, does not have the final say either. Resurrection of the spiritual body is more than either new life in the present or Greek immortality of the imprisoned soul in the human body. Paul's logic is that Christ, who is the "first fruits" (or big brother) in faith, was raised so his brother and sisters in the faith will be raised also (15:42–56).

Chapter 16   Give weekly to the collection for the Jerusalem church (16:1–4). Paul shares his plans to visit. Paul supports his young associate, Timothy, by asking the Corinthians not to despise him (v. 10–11). "Keep alert, stand firm in your faith and be courageous." Do everything in love (v. 13). In the Aramaic language, Paul reverently prays "Our Lord, Come!" (v. 22)

Up Close and Personal:
Identify Different Types of Faith Development

If you wish, write a poem or essay in which you explore the implications of sudden and gradual turnings of the heart to God and to Christ. If you are not a theist, have you experienced moments of self-transcendence, loving regard for others or meaning beyond yourself? Remember that the church in Corinth was the sacred place where followers of Christ grew in relationship to one another and with Christ. Paul had a sudden transformation on the road to Damascus. However, he did not impose the same kind of conversion experience or sudden change of mind and heart on his followers. In 1 Corinthians, salvation is a process of becoming. Salvation as a process is in keeping with Paul's style of deliberation or slow consideration: "For the message about the cross is foolishness to those who are perishing, but to us who are being saved it is the power of God" (1:18). In the first two verses of chapter 15, Paul reminds his hearers of "the good news" in which they "are being saved." The operative word is being. Growing in awareness of the good news of what God did in Jesus is the path of salvation.

Those who want an introduction to William James, who studied various styles of religious experiences, might start with a biography: *Genuine Reality: A Life of William James*, by Linda Simon. See the bibliography for details.

15

The Second Letter to the Corinthians

In Christ, God Reconciled the World to Himself

Overview

BIBLICAL LITERATURE and church life can be messy. I hope that no one asks you to recall how many fragments of letters there could be in 2 Corinthians. I do want you to remember that Paul tried to ease the messy conflict in the Corinthian churches and found strength in weakness.

Paul was strengthened, by God's consolation, to savor and share with other people. Fatigue and fragility shaped his ministry of comfort (4:7—5:10). Consolation led to consoling. Conflict forced him to reflect on God in Christ as reconciler, and to create a ministry of reconciliation (5:11–21).

Finding strength in weakness is a religious experience that bridges the chasms of centuries and cultures. The late Henri Nouwen gave us the phrase "wounded healers," words that describe Paul.[1] Nouwen was a spiritual writer who taught at Harvard and Yale. During the last years of his life, he served at L'Arche, Jean Vanier's community for the developmentally challenged. Wounded people can become healers. A person who has been very sick may help other people who have the same illness. I know a minister who experienced a great deal of ridicule in his childhood family. As a pastor, he has helped others deal with issues of rejection. Sometimes pain is redeemed, or turned into counsel to offer to other people.

---

1. Stackhouse, "Wounded Healers."

The Second Letter to the Corinthians

Background
Fragmented Letter

Second Corinthians is a letter that may be a composite of fragments from several letters. Paul wrote 2 Corinthians to the same congregation addressed in 1 Corinthians and all the saints throughout Achaia. Macedonia is the likely place of composition. Second Corinthians was written around AD 54–56. Thus, Paul wrote 2 Corinthians between his writing of 1 Thessalonians and Romans.[2]

The disjointed nature of this book is confusing. After Paul started the first church in Corinth, he wrote more than one letter to the Corinthians. There are different theories about how many, and exactly where they were written. My understanding of the order of letters is based on the introductory comments by John T. Fitzgerald in the HarperCollins Study Bible.[3] The simplest theory is that Paul wrote a letter (A) to the Corinthians before he wrote the letter known as 1 Corinthians (B). That first letter (A) that was written before 1 Corinthians was lost. Then Paul wrote 1 Corinthians (B). After writing 1 Corinthians, he wrote a "letter of tears" (C) that is referred to in 2 Cor 1:23–2:4 and 7:5–11. This tearful letter was lost, unless part of it is in 2 Cor 10–13. Then Paul wrote 2 Corinthians (D). However, chapters 10–13 may also have been a later letter as well as possibly the lost "letter of tears."

After Paul wrote 1 Corinthians, Timothy went to Corinth. (We know that because of Acts 19:21–22.) There were hostile "false apostles" there who undermined Paul. Then Paul went to Corinth. Someone, possibly the accused man in 1 Corinthians, publicly affronted him and threatened his authority (5:1). Paul went away to cool down. At first he thought he should not visit again, and wrote a letter "with many tears" that was meant to show love, not to give grief. The Corinthians repented, and Paul made a third visit.

Personal Defense and Deepening Theology

Paul had to defend his ministry and authority as an apostle. Conflict with a church forced Paul to develop his theology and argument through letter writing. Paul needed to explain his job description and what it means to live by faith when there is affliction and criticism. He had to patch up hurt feelings over his failure to visit. Above all, Paul's goal was reconcilia-

---

2. Fitzgerald, "Introduction," 2166.
3. Ibid., 2165.

tion and restoration of mutual regard among himself, the church, and the person who mistreated him in a previous visit. In summary, Paul had to persuade the community to regain their earlier regard for him and to keep on taking the collection for the Jerusalem church.

Literary Unity from Mounting Tensions

As we have seen, 2 Corinthians is a fragmented letter. In fact, it goes back and forth between conflict and a spirit of reconciliation. Sometimes Paul sees his congregation as co-workers (1:24), and at other times he seems dictatorial (10:4, 13:10). Paul's tone borders on bullheaded, especially when he describes his opponents. Yet there is a kind of unity in motion as tensions mount and reconciliation becomes more urgent.

Artistic Elements

Perspective

Paul found orientation to eternity by being united with Christ in the beginnings of a new order of creation that offers reconciliation.

High-Contrast Portraits

Paul painted a detailed picture of himself. His self-portrait presents an apostle and pressured church leader who is anxious about his charges (11:28). As an apostle, Paul suffered in order to spread the gospel message and strengthen the emerging Christian fellowships (11:23–27). Paul's hard-earned conviction is that the Lord's power is made perfect in his weakness. He experienced Christ saying to him, "'My grace is sufficient for you, for power is made perfect in weakness'" (12:9).

In contrast to his detailed self-portrait, Paul verbally draws an impressionistic outline of his opponents (the false apostles), and therefore we do not know much about them. He characterizes them as deceitful workers disguising themselves as apostles, and is not entirely clear about the content of their offending beliefs. The contrast between Paul's detailed picture of himself and the sketchy picture of his opponents' traits makes Paul's ministry stand out as exemplary.

The Second Letter to the Corinthians

Colorful Words

Paul, often known for slogans, gives us one that preachers have been using even since Paul came up with it. This colorful phrase taken from chapter 9 verse 7 is "God loves a cheerful giver."

Line

Compared to Paul's writing in Romans and 1 Corinthians, his line of thought in 2 Corinthians is twisty rather than straight. His argument can be divided into two parts that are chapters 1–9 and 10–13.

Text

In chapters 1–9, Paul expressed himself with frankness. (Frank speech becomes boldness in chapters 10–13.) In this first part, Paul identifies himself at the beginning of his letter as "an apostle of Christ Jesus by the will of God" (1:1). Following the greeting, Paul blesses God as the "God of all consolation"(1:3). Paul says that he can pass on the consolation from God that he experienced through suffering. In Asia Paul and fellow Christians were so near death that they learned to rely on God. Dependence opened the way to trust. Paul says that his behavior is guided by grace, not earthly wisdom. Defending himself, he says that at first he decided not to visit Corinth again because his visit would cause pain (2:4). He urges that the offender be shown love. The majority should forgive and console him so he would not have overwhelming sorrow (2:7). In contrast to other leaders, whom he called "peddlers of the word" (2:17), Paul says that he (and Titus) did not need a letter of recommendation because the Corinthian church was his letter (3:1–3). (A present-day parallel would be a pastor's refusing to list references on his resume because the church spoke for itself.) There is freedom where the Spirit of the Lord is present (3:17).

Since it is by God's grace that people are engaged in ministry, they do not lose heart. This treasure of the gospel, Paul tells us, is in clay jars; Paul tells us of the fragile nature of human beings (4:7). Paul maintains that he and his followers were "afflicted but not crushed, struck down but not destroyed" (4:8–9). Paul states his hope that as more people experience grace, there will be more thanksgiving to the glory of God. Paul stresses that "inner nature is being renewed day by day" (4:16). Living by faith means that trouble helps prepare us for glory (4:17).

We should "walk by faith and not by sight" or overconfidence (5:7). In Christ, we are a new creation and reconciled to God: "So if anyone is in Christ, there is a new creation: everything old has passed away; see, everything has become new" (5:17)! Paul believed that his followers were given the mission of spreading the message of reconciliation between God and humanity, and by implication, of finding reconciliation in the church. Since God's appeal came through Gentiles, Christians are ambassadors for Christ (5:17–20).

In chapter 6, using the editorial "we" to suggest a shared ministry, Paul says that the day of salvation is now (vv. 1–2). Turning conventions inside out, Paul and Timothy are, says Paul, "sorrowful but rejoicing, poor but making many rich" (v. 10). "For we are the temple of the Living God" (v. 16). In chapter 7, Paul rejoices at the church's repentance that was a return to God and to right living. He declares confidence in the Corinthians. Because Paul had almost bragged to Titus about the Corinthians, he is relieved by their continued course of faith (vv. 13–16).

In chapter 8, Paul, chair of the first fundraiser in the Christian church, asks for a donation to the Jerusalem collection project. He hopes that the Corinthians will regain their earlier enthusiasm for the project. This offering was from a Gentile Christian church to a mother (Jewish) church. A shared bank account could help cement bonds. (Generally speaking, fundraisers do unite church members through shared tasks.) In his appeal, Paul stresses the example of Christ's generosity (v. 9) and the fair balance between some people's abundance and other people's needs (vv. 13–14). Generosity glorifies God (9:13).

In the second part of 2 Corinthians, conflict between Paul and the church is more intense. Frank speech becomes bold statements—in fact, stronger language than Paul uses in person. Chapters 10–13, which are angrier than the rest of the letter, may be part of a lost letter. Paul defends his ministry against the "super-apostles" (probably the same as the "false apostles," who represented a form of Jewish Christianity). He had firm beliefs about the limits of his mission field and did not believe in comparing his accomplishments with other people's causes for boasting (10:12–18). In chapter 11, Paul's describes his sufferings that give him credibility (vv. 16-30). Then he shares his mystical experience that may have heightened his believability. Through an experience of revelation in Paradise, which is a metaphor for salvation, Paul felt God saying to him, "My grace is sufficient for you, for power is made perfect in weakness" (12:1–9). Paul is able to be content with weakness and hardships for the sake of Christ because when he was weak, he was strong (12:10). Although church workers do deserve to be paid, Paul does not mean to offend the Corinthians by refusing payment. He simply does not want to be a burden. (It is also very possible that he does not want to be beholden to benefactors, which they would likely have been in his culture.) In chapter 13, Paul, asks the Corinthians to examine themselves to see if they are living in the faith (13:5). Paul concludes his letter with a Trinitarian blessing: "The grace of the Lord Jesus Christ, and the love of God, and the communion of the Holy Spirit be with all of you" (13:13).

The World in Front of the Text

A tempera painting, *St. Paul*, which was painted by Konrad von Soest around 1400, is a visual statement of Paul's strength in weakness. St. Paul looks defeated, sad, and wounded. Yet there is strength in the saturated colors of his red and green robe, and in the orange and gold background. These glorious colors may symbolize Paul's potential to turn weakness into a strong, vibrant ministry of reconciliation. This image is in Sister Wendy's *1000 Masterpieces*.[4]

---

4. Beckett, *1000 Masterpieces*, 246.

16

The Letter to the Romans

Justification Comes through Faith and Trust

Background

What Is Romans?

ROMANS IS a theological letter promoting the gospel, and a recommendation of Paul as an apostle and preacher of the gospel message. Unlike Paul's other letters, it does not address a specific churchly problem. This letter was written to God's beloved in Rome, "where Paul had never been but had friends."[1]

Paul's letter is divided into parts that are typical of letters. There is an opening greeting (1:1–7), a prayer of thanksgiving (1:8–15), a statement of theme (1:16–17), theological points (1:18–11:36), ethical advice (12:1–15:13), travel plans (15:22–33), and a conclusion (chapter 16).

By Whom Was Romans Written?

Paul is definitely the author. Before going to Jerusalem to deliver money donated by his churches, he dictated his letter to Tertius (see Rom 16:22). Phoebe probably served as postal transportation clerk by delivering the letter to Rome (see Rom 16:1).

To Whom Was Romans Written?

In a way, Paul spoke to the people in both Jerusalem and Rome. While his letter was addressed to the Romans, Paul also put together his thoughts for the Jerusalem church. His task in Jerusalem was to defend the worth of a largely Gentile church that did not observe Jewish law but was sending money to the Jerusalem church anyway. Although the Roman faith com-

---

1. Brown, *Introduction to the New Testament*, 560.

munity was a mixture of both Jewish and Gentile Christians, he wrote to Christians who were primarily Gentile Christians.[2] Paul also was in some ways preaching or writing to himself as he dealt with his debt to Judaism and also with his distinctive theological insights. In addition to defending Gentile Christianity, Paul needed to defend the continuing worth of Israel in God's plans.

When, Where and Why Was Romans Written?

Paul wrote Romans in AD 57–58. This letter was written in Corinth.[3] As a pastoral theologian, Paul had a pastoral task. His providential mission was to proclaim to the Gentiles the good news of what God had done in Jesus:

> Paul was mainly concerned with the effects or consequences of the gospel: "it is the power of God for the salvation to everyone who has faith . . . in it the righteousness of God is revealed through faith for faith." (1:16–17)[4]

In Paul's thought, both Gentiles and Jews needed help from God because of the power of sin and death. To Paul the domination of sin and death was broken through the death and resurrection of Jesus. As a result, people can share in Jesus's relationship with God by imitating his faithfulness, and can experience justification by faith apart from works of the Mosaic law (Rom 3:28).

Artistic elements

Lens

My understanding since high school has been that Paul's lens is justification by faith, with a focus on the implications for the individual. However, the word *justification* is related to the word *justice*, a word that prompts thought about the social dimensions of justification. Enormously simplifying N. T. Wright in the *New Interpreter's Bible*, I report his view that Romans 1:17 (which states, "the one who is righteous will live by faith" alone) is about covenant faithfulness and justice rather than just about justification.[5] For Paul, the divine purpose for all creation would be revealed through Israel—the covenant people. When God fulfilled the covenant,

---

2. Duling and Perrin, *New Testament*, 239.
3. Brown, *Introduction the New Testament*, 560.
4. Harrington, *Who Is Jesus?* 103.
5. *New Interpreter's Bible*, 10:403.

the Gentiles would know what its "own life was about."[6] I hope the following distillation is fair: For people of faith, like Abraham, whether men and women of the covenant or of the emerging Christian fellowship, life in the Spirit would not mean worship of the government or belief that all justice flows from Rome. My spin is that perhaps it could be said that the gospel is inevitably followed by the social gospel, and life in the spirit is followed by highest allegiance to God who in the end will make the world right for all humanity.

As you can see, the term *justification* is complex, and a shorter definition appears in the list of words that color Paul's letter. One meaning of *justification* is an attribute or characteristic of God. God is just. Another aspect is justice in action, or the power to make evil right or to mend broken relationships. God has the power to heal. Still another dimension of justification is the effect of justification. God effects justification. What are the effects of justification? What happens in people's inner lives when they affirm the justification that comes from Christ's dying for sinners, which ended the need for animal sacrifice as atonement and opened the way for all people to be in a relationship with God? When a person trusts God as Jesus trusted his heavenly Father, what fruits of the spirit mature? A synonym for *justification* is "reconciliation." Another alternative word for *justification* is "acceptance." Acceptance from God for the people we are rather than what callous people with no respect for nature or regard for grace want us to be is a great treasure. Theologian Paul Tillich said, "Simply accept the fact that you are accepted."[7] A feeling of acceptance into the family of God can effect changes in attitude and behavior.

Through his lens of faith, Paul saw new sightings of life in the Spirit. Using legal language of acquittal, Paul had the courage to think about mysteries of darkness and light, of rejection and reception of the new life in Christ. Paul heard the call and came to belong to Christ Jesus, whom he believed offered saving power to the Jews first but also the Greeks. Hospitality, forgiveness, holding fast to the good, and overcoming evil with good (Rom 12:9–21) are part of the new age inaugurated by Christ.

Words that Color Paul's Writing[8]

- *Body*: The whole person; body, mind, and soul.

---

6. *New Interpreter's Bible*, 10:405.

7. Tillich, *Shaking of the Foundations*, 162.

8. The following definitions are based on the section "Paul's Theological Vocabulary" in Harrington, *Romans*, 12–15.

- *Death*: A punishment for sin and also a power that goes with sin and the law.
- *Faith*: Total trust in God that Abraham showed us; "faith of Christ" may mean the trust that Jesus had in God, or faith in Christ. Like Christ, Abraham was willing to place himself in God's hands.
- *Flesh*: The part of a person that is so weak, angry with God, and rebellious that it is opposite of *spirit*.
- *Gentile*: Non-Jews and sometimes also means Gentile Christians.
- *Gospel*: The good news of Jesus Christ and his death, resurrection, and what they opened up for all people. Scholars call this action of God, the *Christ Event*. In brief the gospel for Paul is the "power of God for salvation for everyone who has faith" (Rom 1:16).
- *Justification*: Even before the Last Judgment, justification means that God's acquittal—which suggests clearance or clean slate or fresh file in your computer—makes righteousness possible. *Reconciliation* is very close in meaning.
- *Law*: Usually the Mosaic law or sometimes natural law, which is a natural ability of people to know right from wrong. For Paul, the Mosaic law was good, but it told people what sin is and thus tempted them to not always do right.
- *Righteousness*: God's justice, made clear in Christ, looks forward to a positive statement from God at the Last Judgment. Such anticipation makes possible a new relationship with God.
- *Salvation*: Rescue from moral evil in the present.
- *Sin*: Sometimes wrongdoing and sometimes a strong power linked with death or the law. Basic alienation and failure to recognize absolute dependence upon God are sin in Paul's view.
- *Spirit*: Openness to God in interior places that are touched by the Holy Spirit.
- *World*: Sometimes seen as neither good nor bad, but at other times seen as under the power of sin.

Texture

Paul's use of Old Testament passages gives texture to Romans. The poem in chapter 3, verses 10–18 uses passages from the Old Testament to show that sin is widespread and that every person needs the gospel. This piling up of quotations creates texture. Here are some of the Old Testament ties:

1. Rom 3:10 is a paraphrase of Eccl 7:20.
2. For Rom 3:11–12, see Ps 14:2–3.
3. For Rom 3:13, see Ps 5:9 and Ps 140:3.
4. For Rom 3:14, see Ps 10:7.
5. For Rom 3:15–17, see Isa 59:7–8.
6. For Rom 3:18, see Ps 36:1.

Linear Logic

Romans has two main parts. Part one, chapters 1–11, is a sustained argument for the idea that the only way to satisfy God's demand for righteousness is through faith. Part two, chapters 12–16, is an explanation of the requirements of Christian life. The most important formal quality of Romans is line. Discover Paul's linear logic by following his line of thought chapter by chapter.

Text

Part One: Righteousness through Faith

Chapter 1   The gospel reveals the righteousness of God for every believer, first the Jew, then the Greek. Righteousness of God is revealed through faith (vv.16–17). Gentiles knew God through nature, but they ignored God and did not always behave well. Thus failure to acknowledge God can be the root of sin.

Chapter 2   God does not show partiality and judges according to actions (vv. 6–11). (There is a sense of universality here or a suggestion that God treats all people alike.)

Chapter 3   God entrusted his oracles to the Jews, but God is God for everyone. The law could not do for Paul what Christ did, but it was an important witness. All people have sinned but are justified by faith apart from works prescribed by the law (v. 28), or are justified by a radical trust in God, whether or not they have been circumcised or have kept the law. ("Faith" can mean the faith and trust of Christ, as well as our faith in Christ.)

Chapter 4 Abraham trusted God, and his faith as radical trust, even before circumcision, made him righteous.

Chapter 5 Christ died and lived for us. Reconciliation came from Christ's death, and salvation from his living. We have access to God through faith, and reconciliation through Christ: "For if while we were enemies, we were reconciled to God through the death of his Son, much more surely, having been reconciled, will we be saved by his life" (v. 10). Justification and reconciliation are basically synonymous. The disobedience of Adam causes disaster. Christ obeyed in a grace-filled relationship with his heavenly Father. Christ is the source of blessing we share in new life.

Chapter 6 Our baptism into Christ's death and resurrection means that sin and death no longer control us. This walk in the newness of life is about the future resurrected life as well as life in the present.

Chapter 7 Sin is part of the human condition that prevents us from being our best, unified selves. In an either/or- rather than a both/and attitude, which must have been necessary in the breaking-away-from-Judaism stage of Christianity, Paul questions that validity of the law that made him aware of sin and that, for him, was not helpful. The Spirit gives new life.

Chapter 8 The life-giving law of the Spirit sets people free (v. 2). People who are led by the Spirit are children of God (v. 14). Yearnings for the fullness of God were so pervasive that the whole created universe groaned in waiting (v. 22). First fruits of fulfillment have come from the Spirit. Nothing can separate us from the love of God (vv. 35–39).

Chapter 9 Being children of God depends upon promise and election not just biological heritage. Gentiles obtain righteousness and right relationship with God through faith. Christ is like a master potter (v. 21).

Chapter 10 Christ is the "end" of the law in the sense of its "fulfillment" (v. 4). Faith in the heart means that God is near and salvation is at hand (v. 9). There is no distinction between Jew

PART FOUR: THE REST OF PAUL'S LETTERS

and Greek because the same Lord is generous to all that call upon him (vv. 9–13).

Chapter 11 Paul does not deny his Jewish heritage but sees Jewish Christians as the faithful remnant who providentially respond to Jesus and show that Gentiles can enjoy full membership in the family of God. God's ways are mysterious, so Gentiles should not be overconfident. God has not ultimately rejected Israel, but has grafted Gentiles onto the family tree (vv. 23–24). God's call to Israel is irrevocable (v. 29).

Part Two: The Requirements of New Life

Chapter 12 New life in Christ means renewal, discerning the will of God, participating in the body of Christ by modestly sharing spiritual gifts, persevering in prayer, loving the genuine, practicing hospitality, blessing those who persecute you, and showing concern for enemies (vv. 1–20). "Do not be overcome by evil, but overcome evil with good" (v. 21).

Chapter 13 Love fulfills the law (v. 8), so pay taxes and fulfill the law through loving your neighbor as yourself. (The government at the time was fairly friendly, so of course Paul advised civil obedience. By the time the book of Revelation was written, the authorities were hostile. So different social situations call forth different views and sometimes new duties.)

Chapter 14 In contrast to harshly judging others, pursue peace and mutual building up of the communities. The kingdom of God, a concept Paul rarely uses, is about righteousness, peace, and joy in the Holy Spirit (v. 17). Pursue those things that please neighbors and make for peace.

Chapter 15 Paul prays and pleads for harmony. His prayer, which is embedded in narrative, is:

May the God of steadfastness and encouragement grant you to live in harmony with one another, in accordance with Christ Jesus, so that together you may with one voice glorify the God and Father of our Lord Jesus Christ. (vv. 5–7)

"Welcome one another . . . as Christ . . . welcomed" us. Christ welcomed all so that the Gentiles might glorify the God of hope and mercy (vv. 7–9), A fundraiser for the poor people in Jerusalem could unify the Roman church through team effort, and could diplomatically affirm the blessings and spiritual treasures of Israel (v. 28).

Chapter 16 Paul's final greetings, which may be an addition, were addressed to a lively group of men and women in a warm and appreciative manner. He mentions Phoebe, a deacon in a sister church; Prisca and Acquila, who were a married couple and church workers. Paul also notes Junia, whom he considered an apostle; Rufus's mother and Paul's spiritual mother (v. 13); as well as the city treasurer, Erastus (v. 23). Paul's wish that his associates avoid deceivers and be wise about what is good also serves parish councils well today. Greet one another, avoid dissension. "The grace of our Lord Jesus Christ be with you" (v. 20).

The World in Front of the Text
Reflective Activities

1. Read or reread Romans 3:21–27. The concept of atonement is a difficult theological concept. The word *atonement*, broken up, suggests the most basic meaning: at-one-ment. Put most simply, Jesus's life, sacrificial death, and resurrection opened up religious life and made it possible for people to be at one with God. Atonement language describes and defines adoption. In Romans 8, those who have been lead by the Spirit have received a spirit of adoption and call God "Father." Can you write one paragraph describing a time when you felt at one with God or when you knew that you belong to God?

2. Read or reread Romans 8. This chapter is a powerful promise of God's love. When I was a senior in high school, an unusually high number of classmates lost a parent in death. With each sympathy note, I included verses from Romans. Perhaps you would like to write out those verses or type them on your computer. When a friend needs a reminder of God's presence, you can give a copy of verses from Romans. The verses I used from Romans 8 are verses 31b, 35, and 37–39:

   - If God is for us, who is against us?
   - Who will separate us from the love of Christ? Will hardship, or distress, or persecution, or famine, or nakedness, or peril, or sword?

- No, in all these things we are more than conquerors through him who loved us. For I am convinced that neither death, nor life, nor angels, nor rulers, nor things present, nor things to come, nor powers, nor height, nor depth, nor anything else in all creation, will be able to separate us from the love of God in Christ Jesus our Lord.

3. Consider different understandings: Scholars and pastors, teachers and evangelists, have discussed and argued Paul's points and proclamation in Romans. What is so important about this book? The answers depend upon whom you ask. Ask a Lutheran, and you will likely hear, "Justification by faith alone." Ask one of my former classmates at Weston Jesuit School of Theology, and she or he might say that Paul's understanding of Gentiles being grafted onto the family tree of Judaism was Paul's brilliant theological solution to the problem of how Jews and Christians are related. A Protestant on the far left might respond, "I do not care about Paul. My interest is Jesus of the Synoptic Gospels."

Well, loosen up, folks. These divergent views are not as incompatible as they might seem. Grace and graft and gospel are connected. Pared to the core, the following distilled definitions are based on Paul's thought, plus the continuing history of Christian spirituality. Grace is experienced in tasting God's abiding love and knowing that the sweetness of joy will remain. Graft is organic bonding onto God's family tree. Gospel is the good news of God's outreach to humanity through the life, death, and resurrection of Jesus.

Because the gospel is the focal point, Romans is sometimes referred to as "the Gospel according to Paul." For Paul, the "good news" or gospel is Jesus Christ. Paul wrote that "the gospel concerning [God's] Son, who was descended from David . . . was declared to be the Son of God . . . through whom we have received grace" (Rom 1:3–5). The main theme, like a focal point in a painting, is found in chapter 1 verses 16–17:

> For I am not ashamed of the gospel; it is the power of God for salvation to everyone who has faith, to the Jew first and also to the Greek. For in it the righteousness of God is revealed through faith for faith; as it is written, "The one who is righteous will live by faith."

The spirituality of Romans chapter 12 that includes concern for enemies is in keeping with the Jesus of the Synoptic Gospels, especially with the Sermon on the Mount in Matthew 5–7.

Art Activity: Faces of Grace That Inspire Faith

Make a collage picture of faces that symbolize God's grace to you and have helped you have faith. (A collage is anything glued to paper or board.) Think about the faces of people you know, and those you do not know, who suggest love, patience, friendliness, concern, acceptance, welcome, or understanding. Is there a person in your life who trustingly put himself or herself into God's hands? We have not seen God's face, but faces of *people* can be symbols of God's face and bearing to us. Collect pictures of faces that suggest kindness and grace. You could cut faces from old magazines or newspapers, or photocopy faces from books. If you are Christian, you might want to use a picture of Christ in your collage. Whatever your beliefs are, you could use pictures of people who help you feel that ultimately the world is friendly and that nothing can separate us from love in the heart of the cosmos.

17

The Letter to Philemon
Christian Love Kindles Kindred Bonds

ALLITERATION IS a way to remember. Philemon is a phenomenal picture of *philadelphia* that in New Testament Greek, as in the name of the city, means "brotherly or sisterly love."

Background
A Short Letter

Philemon is a short, persuasive letter that was written in AD 55, probably in Ephesus.[1] Martin Luther said it gives us a tender illustration of Christian love.[2] Paul is definitely the author. He wrote to Philemon, Apphia, Archippus, and the church that met in Philemon's house. Writing in prison as a prisoner who had sacrificed his freedom for Christ, Paul requested freedom for a runaway slave named Onesimus.

Artistic Elements
Perspective

Being a new creation gave Paul the perspective to see that in Christ all are brothers and sisters. Paul wanted freedom for the escaped slave, Onesimus, who was his convert in prison. In Paul's day, slaves were not treated as brutally as slaves were in pre-Civil-War America. Slavery was not based on race, and slaves were more like servants in nineteenth-century England. In Roman culture, as in England portrayed in the television series *Upstairs, Downstairs*, society was very stratified.[3] Moving into another class was

---

1. Brown, *Introduction to the New Testament*, 503.
2. *New Interpreter's Bible*, 11:886 cites Eduard Lohse, *Colossians and Philemon*, 188; Lohse, in turn, cites Martin Luther on Philemon.
3. Brown, *Introduction to the New Testament*, 504.

most unusual. Thus, Paul's plea that Philemon free Onesimus was indeed a new thing that grew out of being a new creation in Christ. The power to transform lives is witness to abiding truth. We can assume Paul's request was honored, or we would not likely have the story of Philemon and Onesimus in the New Testament.

Focal Point

The focal point is love in action or as Paul put it, "all the good that we may do for Christ" (Phlm 6).

The Text in the Middle Ground

This letter has divisions, which are typical features of Paul's letters. These divisions are identification of the sender, thanksgiving to God, body of the letter, final greetings, and benediction. Paul addresses his letter to Philemon and also the entire house church. Apphia was likely Philemon's wife. Archippus might have been a son, co-worker, or minister of the house church. The key phrase in Paul's thanksgiving to God is, "your love for all the saints" (v. 5), or the mutual Christian love among church members. Paul appeals to Philemon on the basis of love. He could have been an advocate for Onesimus under Roman law. Verse 6 is intercessory prayer. "My prayer is that your fellowship with us in our common faith may deepen the understandings of all the blessings that our union with Christ brings us" (*New English Bible*). Paul, who has been encouraged by love, appeals to Philemon's love in his letter from prison. This love is deeply felt inwardly in the heart.

Paul's writing to a whole church brings pressure on Philemon to respond positively to Paul's request to accept back the runaway slave, Onesimus. Exactly why Onesimus left is a matter of conjecture. His only offense may have been a desire to get away from abuse. While he was in prison, Paul converted and nurtured Onesimus. He praised the members of the house church for their love and faith. He gently asserts his authority by reminding his readers that his is a prisoner for Christ as well as an old man. Paul asks Philemon to accept Onesimus back as a brother. Paul implies that he might like Philemon to send Onesimus back to him to be a co-worker. Paul says, "So if you consider me your partner, welcome him as you would welcome me" (v. 17). The word *partner* suggests kinship. A present-day hymn that matches the spirit of this request is "Blessed Be the Tie That Binds." The line of the hymn that reads, "Our hearts in Christian love" expresses Christian bonds. Allowing for the possibility that Onesimus might have done something wrong, Paul tells Philemon to charge his own account. Paul expects to be released from prison and requests a guestroom. Concluding words are benediction.

In summary, Raymond E. Brown says that Paul's request that Philemon voluntarily receive back a slave challenged Philemon to defy convention and to acknowledge his own transformation.[4]

There is a nice story that Edgar J. Goodspeed heard from scholars before him. The story continues to be reported in current books about the New Testament including *An Introduction to the New* Testament by Father Raymond E. Brown.[5] Forty or fifty years after Paul wrote this letter, Ignatius the bishop of Antoich wrote a letter to the Ephesian church and had much to say about their bishop named Onesimus.[6] We do not know for sure if a former slave, Onesimus, went on to become a bishop. The very possibility is inspiring.

The World in Front of the Text

Looking at Art

Mary, Jesus and two angels are framed in a circle of yellow and white flowers in a glazed terra-cotta: *Madonna and Child between Two Angels* (1475–1480) by Luca della Robbia. This image, to my mind, symbolizes inclusive Christian fellowship with Jesus and Mary as central figures.[7]

Doing Your Own Art

Using a compass, or by tracing a dish, draw a circle on any-sized paper. Paste your own designs or cut out pictures of flowers or leaves or people on the circle. You might wish to put inside the circle a cross; a picture of your church, of Mary and Jesus, or of people engaged in social action.

---

4. Brown, *An Introduction to the New Testament*, 506.
5. Ibid., 508–9.
6. Goodspeed, *Introduction to the New Testament*, 121.
7. *Art Book*, 391.

18

The Letter to the Philippians
Rejoice in the Lord
The Peace of God Will Guard Your Hearts

Background
What Is Philippians?

PHILIPPIANS IS a letter with the customary greeting, body, and closing benediction. In contrast to the calm reasoning in Romans, Paul wrote this letter with warmth and affection. Thus, it is possible that the rough transitions between parts in the body are a result of passionate, flowing thought with emotional rather than logical ordering. Yet the letter may be a compilation of two or three Pauline letters. Compilation would explain why the thank-you note is at the end rather than the more likely beginning of a letter. We cannot know everything about Paul's situation, but he may have thanked the Philippians on a previous occasion for their gift, so that he did not need to mention it first in his letter. Whether this letter was written all at once or compiled from shorter pieces, Philippians is a letter of joy and thanksgiving. This beautiful letter stresses rejoicing, unity in community, sharing in the mind of Christ through service, and openness to sacramental suffering. Fidelity in relationship to God and gentleness in human relationships are guiding ideals.

Within the letter there are other forms of writing including a prayer and a hymn-prayer. (The Psalms in the Old Testament are sometimes called "the prayer book of the Bible" because many psalms are prayers. These prayers are in units that stand by themselves.) Sometimes prayers in the Bible are part of the story or text. One such embedded prayer is found in Phil 1:9–10: "And this is my prayer, that your love may overflow more and more with knowledge and full insight to help you determine what is best, so that in the day of Christ you may be pure and blameless."

When and Where Was Philippians written?

Philippians was written around AD 56 if it was written from Ephesus, or around 61 or 61 if it was written from Rome, or around 58–60 if it was written from Caesarea.[1] Raymond E. Brown has said that there is "no way to decide this issue; but the best arguments seem to be on the side of Ephesus."[2]

Paul wrote this letter in prison and included Timothy as cosender. He wrote to the Christian community at Philippi. Philippi was a small city of about ten thousand people. It was situated on the main road, Via Egnatia. Since this city was a Roman colony, citizens had many property and legal rights without the heavy taxes imposed on people who lacked status. The official language was Latin. Paul's converts there were almost all from families of Gentile origin.[3]

Artistic Elements

Perspective

Christians participate in Christ by following his example of obedience and humble service. The idea of living like Christ is woven throughout the New Testament and comes to fullest expression in Philippians.

Color Word

The word *joy* colors the text. Paul prays with joy because the Philippians as a community shared the gospel (1:3). Paul notes the Philippians' *joy in faith* (1:25). In his plea for unity of mind, Paul wants the Philippians to "make my joy complete: be of the same mind, having the same love, being in full accord and of one mind" (2:2).

Focal Point

Two words, *essence* and *exaltation*, express the core of Paul's thought in Philippians. The historical Jesus's essence was service to God. In Paul's thought, Jesus as the risen Christ and Lord is exaltation.

---

1. Brown, *Introduction to the New Testament*, 484.
2. Ibid., 496.
3. *New Interpreter's Bible*, 11:469–71 by Morna D. Hooker.

The Letter to the Philippians

Movement within the Letter

The movement of the letter expresses Paul's affection for his people and his hopes for their spiritual development. In contrast to his role of pastoral theologian when writing Romans, Paul, writing Philippians from prison, is more like an online teacher or spiritual advisor. The movement is not the linear logic of Romans but a prayerful movement that suggests either a retreat or summer church camp or a special Sunday evening worship service with the theme of becoming more Christlike. We can imagine that someone read the Letter to the Philippians for Paul, and that his listeners thoughtfully pondered the message.

Line of the Text

The general outline starts with Paul and Timothy addressing the people; he called *all the saints* (1:1), who were members of a church he founded in Philippi. Timothy is not a co-writer. He is included as a courtesy. Paul and Timothy are identified as "servants," and this designation foreshadows the hymn in chapter 2 that sings of Christ taking the form of a servant. In his salutation, Paul mentions the bishops and deacons who are with the saints in Philippi. While it is important to know that the early church had these leaders, the bishops and deacons are not exactly like they are today. These bishops and deacons strike me as being like Methodist district superintendents.

In the first chapter, Paul rejoices with the Philippians as they rejoice with him. He longs for the Philippians "with the compassion of Christ Jesus" (1:8). He prays that the Philippians will have love that overflows with "knowledge and insight" that help them discern what is best so that in the day of Christ they will be "pure and blameless" (1:9–11). In other words, Paul wants them to distinguish the things that matter. He believes that his imprisonment helped spread the gospel because even the imperial guard took note (1:13). Paul will continue to rejoice that Christ is proclaimed, and Paul knows that prison will turn out to be about his deliverance (1:19). For Paul, living means fruitful labor and being around for the people who need him. Dying means being more fully with Christ in the resurrected life. He asks his followers to live in a manner worthy of the gospel (1:27).

In chapter 2, Paul asks the Philippians to make his joy complete by having unity of mind and love. Unity here does not refer to intellectual thought but to having a common attitude. A hymn within the letter stresses the form of Christ, which is the essence of Jesus's life and love. Paul's joy will be complete if his flock finds encouragement in Christ and responds in the spirit of the hymn:

> Let the same mind be in you that was in Christ Jesus, who, though he was in the form of God, did not regard equality with God as something to be exploited, but emptied himself, taking the form of a slave, being born in human likeness. And being found in human form, he humbled himself and became obedient to the point of death—even death on a cross. Therefore God also highly exalted him and gave him the name that is above every name, so that at the name of Jesus every knee should bend, in heaven and on earth and under the earth, and every tongue should confess that Jesus Christ is Lord, to the glory of God the Father. (Phil 2:5–11)

This hymn was likely one that Paul knew from Christian worship and quoted, and therefore it tells us something about early Christian beliefs about Jesus.[4] It does seem to me that this passage might also be a prayer or confession of faith. I can imagine Christians at the time and worshipers today kneeling in either body or spirit when hearing the words "every knee should bend." Generally, it seems to me that the Bible is a book of faith, not creeds. Yet this passage comes as close to a credo as it gets. An important theological point is that the biblical hymn shows that at an early stage of Christian history, Jesus was understood as sharing God's form. Still it needs to be said that the historical context was about Christian living. To my mind, this passage seems to imply that Jesus is less than is God the Father. New Testament authors did not write with sensitivities to future debates and church councils. As Morna D. Hooker points out, Paul was not as interested in the finer points of the divine and human natures of Jesus as were the Church Fathers of the fourth and fifth centuries.[5] Yet, certainly this hymn is the beginning of reflection on the nature and mission of Christ.

Many Christians see this passage as a statement of Christ's preexistence and therefore emphasize the interpretation that Jesus was preexistent or with God from the very start. Other Christians see a reference to Israel as the suffering servant and therefore stress the importance of Jesus's taking the form of a slave like the Suffering Servant in Isaiah. (Jesus's example of sacrificial love as the subject of the Philippians Christ hymn was clearly the emphasis during my college days.) Still others understand Christ as the new Adam who, unlike the first Adam, did not try to be equal with God.

---

4. Harrington, *Paul's Prison Letters*, 47.
5. *New Interpreter's Bible*, 11:476.

Whatever a person's view, one feature that invites consensus is that Jesus did not exploit his connections to God.

In any case, an important word is *therefore*. This word marks the transition or change from the essence of humility to exaltation in God. This passage is both about Christ, and about how those in Christ should live. In this hymn, celebration is singing about the lordship of Christ over all creation. Knees bend in heaven and on earth in response to Christ's living with love and loving with death. The example of Christ's love inspires good behavior. Being conformed to Christ means striving to live a Christlike life. The prayerful, reflective qualities of this hymn can draw thoughtful worshippers into a receptive mood that welcomes the mind of Christ. Entering into Christ's frame of mind keeps Christ's followers growing in trust, obedience and service.

The combination prayer, hymn, and confession of faith flows into spiritual direction or exhortation:

> Therefore, my beloved, just as you have always obeyed me, not only in my presence, but much more now, in my absence, work out your own salvation with fear and trembling; for it is God who is at work in you, enabling you both to will and to work for his good pleasure. Do all things without murmuring and arguing, so that you may be blameless and innocent, children of God without blemish in the midst of a crooked and perverse generation, in which you shine like stars in the world. (Phil 2:12–14)

The words "crooked and perverse generation" are from Deuteronomy 32:5. This quotation adds texture or a layer of meaning by alluding to Moses' song and possibly suggesting a farewell address. We do not know for sure the identity of the people of a "crooked and perverse generation." However, the Philippians—as children of God aligned with God—would not be crooked. "Shining like stars" in the darkness of a perverse world (2:15) echoes Matthew's stress on Jesus's instruction on being the light of the world (Matt 5:14). Paul rejoices that his helper Epaphroditus has recovered from almost fatal illness (2:25–30).

In chapter 3, Paul summarizes his impeccable track record as a Hebrew but views former gains as losses in comparison to the supreme value of knowing Christ Jesus (3:7–10). Paul's values have changed from faith in the Mosaic law (3:6) to faith in Christ's fidelity to his Father as the example of right relationship with God (3:9–11).

Using an athletic image, Paul states, "I press on toward the goal for the prize of the heavenly call of God in Christ Jesus" (3:14). Then, using a political image, Paul tells his readers that they are citizens of heaven (3:20). Dual citizenship on earth and in heaven is a metaphor the Philippians would have understood because they held dual citizenship in their city and Rome. Citizenship is a communal concept, which reinforces unity.

Paul winds down his online course or summer church camp, or concludes his worship service (or in more traditional terms starts to end his letter). Paul calls his brothers and sisters his *joy* and *crown* in chapter 4. He urges two women to be of the same mind in the Lord. We do not know what the issue was between Euodia and Syntyche. As in many churchly disagreements, the matter was likely forgotten or deemed inconsequential compared to the greater good of unity. Paul encourages gentleness and rejoicing, and he guides his flock in how to pray:

> Rejoice in the Lord always; again I will say "Rejoice." Let your gentleness be known to everyone. The Lord is near. Do not worry about anything, but in everything by prayer and supplication with thanksgiving your requests be made known to God. And the peace of God, which surpasses all understanding, will guard your hearts and your minds in Christ Jesus. (4:4–7)

Prison gives Paul a real-life values clarification game. He has plenty of time to think about the qualities that make life decent and holy. His own prayer for discernment at the beginning of his letter is answered in his own life. Out of his own experience, reflection, and discernment he directs others to rejoice in the Lord and to think about whatever is true, honorable, just, and pure (4:8). Paul thanks the Philippians for helping out when he was in Thessalonica and ends with a benediction (4:16–23).

The World in Front of the Text

Reflecting on Service

Paul instructed the Christians of his day to shine like stars in the world (Phil 2:15). Similarly, Jesus said in Matthew 5:14, "You are the light of the world." Think about how you can be more Christlike and shine to God's glory by giving back to God and life.

Looking at Art

The following exploration of Georges Rouault's crucifixion as a personal, painterly prayer is based on Soo Yun Kang's summary description of a series of Rouault's prints entitled *Miserere* as a "prayer book of hope."[6] Georges Rouault was an early-twentieth-century painter and printmaker. From an early age, he saw human suffering and often painted the poor, and Christ in his passion. Without regarding the poor as sinless, biblical verses paired with almost iconic images of downtrodden, vulnerable people import empathy, promise of God's presence in the present, and future consolation.

Rouault's crucifixion scene (plate 57 in Flora and Kang) titled with a phrase from Philippians *Obedient unto death, even the death of the Cross* (Translated from the French by Soo Yun Kang) is prayerful recognition of Christ's sacrificial love. This evocative image honors Christ's obedience, passion, and service and offers invitation to meet Christ in his suffering and to find hope in returning to God. Reflection on this confessional, painterly prayer may enable viewers to embrace their own suffering and find their own forms of service.

---

6. See Flora and Kang, *Georges Rouault's "Miserere et guerre,"* 44; see bibliography for further details. You can order this book from the Museum of Biblical Art in New York.

Part Five

Cosmic Christ Served by Good Deeds and Growing Ministry

19

The Letter to the Colossians
Christ, the Wisdom of God, Is All in All

Six words introduce and summarize Colossians. These six words in three phrases are: 1. Colossal Church; 2. Cosmic Christ; and 3. Congregational Chorus.

1. Colossal Church: In this letter the church is becoming a more structured institution. Eventually, the organized institution will be a colossal church with Christ as the head.
2. Cosmic Christ: Christ is seen as the true representation of God. The body of Christ is not just the church but a cosmic reality (1:18, 24; 2:19; 3:15).
3. Congregational Chorus: In time many churches will be a worldwide congregational chorus affirming the Christ hymn in Colossians 1:15–20.

Background
Prison Letter

Colossians is a letter with a prison setting that was probably written in Paul's name by a disciple to Gentile Christians in Colossae, who were members of a church not founded by Paul. Colossians was written in Ephesus no later than AD 80 and maybe earlier.

Development of Paul's Thought

About 60 percent of critical scholars believe that Paul did not write Colossians.[1] The strongest case for a letter written in Paul's name by a faithful follower to address a new situation is a theological argument. The

---

1. Brown, *Introduction to the New Testament*, 600.

very precise statement in the hymn in chapter 1 verses 15–23 that Christ is the "head" of the church (1:18) goes beyond Paul's understanding of the church in the letters he definitely wrote. (I will sometimes refer to the author as Paul, whom the writer described as both "apostle" [1:1] and "servant" [1:24].)

Orthodox Thought and Location of Wisdom

Paul warned Gentile Christians again about the dangers of false teachers who might have endorsed a form of esoteric Judaism that emphasized fasting and visionary experiences. The author wrote to a very specific situation. His advice should not be seen as condemning all forms of Judaism or ascetic practices. The author instructed his readers and hearers to avoid vices such as anger, malice, and slander and to practice virtues such as compassion, kindness, and patience (3:8–12).

Most important, he showed that personified Wisdom is in Christ. He stressed the superiority of Christ over principalities and powers (2:15). No elements in the universe have any power over the Colossians because Christ has taken them away from the powers of darkness into his realm (1:14). The author's viewpoint is that Christ is the full embodiment of God, and "in him all things hold together" (1:17). God's "treasures of wisdom and knowledge" are in Christ (2:3), who is the basis of Christian life. Christ is more powerful than the physical elements of the universe (2:8–15).

Derivative Metaphor Is Focal Point

An artistic metaphor that is derived from the text is Christ as Cosmic Glue. Wisdom in Christ holds all things together. Faith can be an adhesive that binds a community together. For the Colossians, belief in Christ's power was spiritual glue.

Text

Part 1: Theological Statements

Chapter 1

Paul greets the saints in Colossae. He thanks God for their faith in Christ Jesus and their love that they have for "all the saints, because of the hope laid up for you in heaven" (1:4–5). He prays that his followers, who align themselves with the power of light, will live in ways pleasing to God and bear fruit as they grow in the knowledge of God (1:10). Verses 15 to 23 are a hymn about the supremacy Christ. Finding richness in Judaism, the author expands a familiar motif of personified wisdom. Drawing upon Proverbs 8 and Sirach 24, the author finds Wisdom in Christ, who holds all things together like glue. In this Colossian hymn, Christ is the image of the invisible God, existing before anything else: the one for whom and through whom creation took place. Christ is the head of the church (1:18). In Christ the fullness of God "was pleased to dwell" (1:19). As the hymn "Amazing Grace" also testifies, people who were once estranged from God are reconciled with God through Christ. God has made known to the Gentiles the mystery of "Christ in you" (1:27). ("Christ in you" means Christ's presence in the church.) The goal of preaching is to let everyone know that they can have a mature or right relationship with God. "It is he whom we proclaim, warning everyone and teaching everyone in all wisdom, so that we may present everyone mature in Christ" (1:28).

Chapter 2

The author wants people to have knowledge of God's mystery, Christ himself:

> I want their hearts to be encouraged and united in love, so that they may have all the riches of assured understanding and have the knowledge of God's mystery, that is, Christ himself, in whom are hidden all the treasures of wisdom and knowledge. (2:2–3)

The writer wants his readers to continue living their lives in Christ and to remain "established" in their faith as they were taught (2:7). He assures his readers that the Christian life is not reduced to the details of observances, overly austere practices, or worship of angels (2:8–19).

Part 2: Ethics

Chapter 3

New life in Christ means being clothed in virtues of "compassion, kindness, humility, gentleness and patience" (3:12) and also means showing mutual respect in human relationships. Fathers should not provoke their children because provoked children may lose heart (3:21). Get rid of malice and abusive language. In the renewal of life in Christ, there is no longer Greek or Jew, circumcised or uncircumcised, slave or free. Barriers of social standing fall away. Christ is all and in all. Household rules, although patriarchal, show mutual regard and responsibility.

Chapter 4

"Devote yourselves to prayers" (4:2). The author sees contacts with outsiders as missionary opportunities and tells Christians to choose their words with the needs of people in mind. Speech should be gracious and "seasoned with salt" (4:6); that is, appropriate for the listeners. He extends greetings and benediction: "Grace be with you" (4:18).

The World in Front of the Text

The household code in chapter 3 verses 18–25 presents problems. Unfortunately, this passage has been used to justify both slavery and domestic abuse. Slavery was part of the culture in which this letter was written and is not acceptable today. This letter must not be used to condone domestic abuse. The advice to treat slaves justly and fairly in light of our common Master in heaven may reflect higher standards than the usual ways of behaving in the secular world of the time. Women in this letter do not have the equality seen in other Pauline letters. Still, husbands are told to never treat their wives harshly. Basic consideration transcends cultures and could be considered a constant ingredient in marriages. The concept of living in God also transcends time and place. We have to decide what parts of this household code are permanent and what parts are from another time and place. Even if we cannot accept the notion that wives should be subject to husbands, is it possible to see positive aspects in this code? How do you feel about the advice to fathers?

Hope on the Horizon

Think about the lovely phrase, "Hope laid up for you in heaven" (1:5).

> The situations and themes included in 1:3–8 provide rich themes of actualization: the practice of thanking God and praying on behalf of other Christians, the importance of faith and hope in Christian life, the cosmic and dynamic nature of the gospel, and hope as the horizon for Christian existence.[2]

Draw a horizon line on a piece of paper. Write the word "hope" on the line. Think about the people or social action programs that inspire hope for you personally or for the future of your faith community or for the ecological well-being of the earth or for economic justice with food for all. Sketch images or jot down words and phrases. Keep images and words for future reference or use right away in a picture, essay, or poem.

2. Harrington, *Paul's Prison Letters*, 84.

20

The Letter of James
Be God's Friends by Being Doers of the Word

Background
What Is James, and to Whom Was It Written?

JAMES IS something like a sermon or homily in the form of a general letter. Yet, James is better understood as a wisdom instruction.[1] Because wisdom is very cosmopolitan or possessed by many different kinds of people, the thoughts in James reflect Hellenistic or Greek moral philosophy as well as the Old Testament book, Proverbs, which may have in my imaginative conjecture been the author's favorite Old Testament Scripture. The Christian movement drew upon sources in the environment and created moral teachings of its own. James, like some other ancient writings, is concerned with "the practical wisdom of right behavior."[2] One estimated date for the book of James is AD 80–90, if this writing as understood as pseudonymous or penned in the name of James, as most scholars conclude.[3] If James the brother of Jesus wrote this letter, an estimated date is before AD 62.[4]

This general letter or wisdom teaching was written somewhere in the eastern Mediterranean world to a general audience for a general situation—to a situation so universal, in fact, that this writing seems contemporary and ecumenical. The address to "the twelve tribes" (1:1) may not be literal but may rather address "a certain 'brand' of Christians quite loyal to the heritage of Israel,"[5] and who were therefore "quite conservative in

---

1. Harrington, *Who Is Jesus?* 159.
2. *New Interpreter's Bible*, 11:179.
3. Harrington, *Who is Jesus?* 160.
4. Ibid., 160.
5. Brown, *Introduction to the New Testament*, 739.

their appreciation of Judaism."[6] Of course, the quality of loyalty and an appreciation of traditions would have applied to the brother of Jesus. The first Christians to hear or read this letter identified with their Jewish roots and Jesus the wise teacher as portrayed in the book of Matthew. James probably had a source of sayings that was something like the Q source of Jesus's sayings that Matthew quoted. Consider one textural example of similar phrasing. In James 4:4, James wrote that "friendship with the world in enmity towards God." Similarly, Matthew wrote in Matt 6:24 that "you cannot serve God and wealth."

Who Wrote James?

James was written by a spiritual brother, or possibly a biological brother, of Jesus. A few scholars continue to believe that James the brother of Jesus wrote this letter, while others think that a disciple who admired James because James was a Christian who was loyal to Judaism wrote this letter. These scholars argue that the Greek is very polished.[7] A person whose first language was a Semitic language would not likely have written that quality of Greek. The book of James only mentions Jesus twice (1:1; 2:1), which does not suggest that the author had a brotherly relationship with Jesus.

The debate over whether or not James the brother of Jesus authored the Letter of James is an issue of high contrasts in viewpoints. The most extraordinary claim I have read about early authorship, that could suggest the brother of Jesus as author, comes from Peter J. Gomes. He writes: "Recent scholarship places the Epistle of James as first by date, followed by I Thessalonians."[8] While I am doubtful because I cannot find direct support for his view, there could be very early material in James's fine contribution to New Testament literature. In his introduction to the Letter of James in the *New Interpreter's Bible*, Luke Timothy Johnson, without claiming that first-generation writing was proof of Jesus's brother as author of James, says: "The position that James is a first-generation writing has much to recommend it." He goes on to mention that "James makes use of Jesus traditions at a stage earlier than their incorporation into the synoptic Gospels."[9] It seems to me that current interest in the noncanonical collection of wisdom sayings known as *The Gospel of Thomas* indicates a need to find the earli-

---

6. Ibid., 726.
7. Ibid., 741.
8. Gomes, *Good Book*, 16.
9. *New Interpreter's Bible*, 11:183.

est forms of Jesus's sayings. If my assessment is correct, I believe that the discussion of James's authorship and time of writing will continue.

In any case, the author of James was a conservative Jewish Christian leader who was very loyal to observing the law. Whether or not James the brother of Jesus wrote the book, the letter reflects traditional beliefs and piety. The author was not completely against Paul but wanted to correct what to his mind was an exaggerated interpretation of Christian freedom. If people in James's day had had cars and bumper stickers, James might have had a sticker based on chapter 2, verse 12 that would have said *Law of liberty*. He cared about the law not as ritual requirement but as moral law summarized as the royal law of love of neighbor as self (2:8). This conservative slogan was, "so speak and so act as those who are to be judged by the law of liberty" (2:12). This rallying cry suggests that for James there was not a dichotomy or split between Christian freedom and some observance of traditional Jewish customs. Older ways of being holy that included close attention to the first five books of the Bible, known as the Torah, continued to help James's community draw close to God, as Jesus did, through purity, piety, and prayer.

Why Was James Written?

The author wanted to persuade his community of readers to live up to their profession of faith in "our glorious Lord Jesus Christ" (2:1). He wanted them to translate their faith into action and was concerned about practical wisdom that is interconnected with right behavior.

Artistic Elements

Counterbalancing Themes

James is about work that flows naturally from faith. The book of Romans is about faith that can fuel work. Therefore the emphases on faith in Romans and on work in James counterbalance and enrich the other.

Texture

James's use of the Old Testament gives his thought continuity and substance, a richness and texture. James drew upon the Old Testament book Leviticus, a source that Matthew also used: "You shall not take vengeance or bear a grudge against any of your people, but you shall love your neighbor as yourself: I am the Lord" (Lev 19:18). In some ways, James is exploration, explanation, and elaboration of the many implications of

Lev 19:18. Like Matthew's Jesus, who came to fulfill the law, the author of James stresses the role of fulfillment: "You do well if you really fulfill the royal law according to the scripture, 'You shall love your neighbor as yourself'" (2:8). Similarly, Matthew 22:39 states: "And a second is like it: 'You should love your neighbor as yourself.'"

Perspective

The perspective is that religion has practical applications. Actions bring happiness, and getting along with others is important. God-given wisdom is open to reason and bears the fruit of mercy and kindly deeds.

Use of Line Contrasts with Line in Romans

James and Romans have different styles of lines. Romans is written in a straight line of linear logic. The writing in James proceeds by emotional and impressionistic associations of themes. James's main idea conveyed by his line of thought is that Christian service completes faith.

The organization line of James is like a string of fine pearls with a golden clasp that holds the necklace together. The string or line is the theme of friendship with God. In the author's understanding, friendship with God means being saved from the world's poison of envy and competition, and turning towards community, cooperation, caring, and contributing to the needy. The individual pearls of wisdom are little sermons that combine to make one longer sermon about friendship with God. The golden clasp is found in chapter 1, verse 27. This verse states that "pure religion is caring for orphans and widows in distress." Such caring illustrates how Christian service completes faith.

Polished pearls of wisdom are very much like the form of short wisdom sayings in Proverbs. Proverbs in the Old Testament, like James in the New Testament, is a book of wisdom instructions. James is something like other ancient world writings that are about practical wisdom or right behavior. However, James is more concerned with morals than with manners.[10] Echoing the teachings of Jesus, the author is concerned for all people—not just the important ones. Jill, who participated in my adult New Testament class, observed that James unlike a string of pearls, will never lose its luster. Her glowing recommendation continues to refresh me after too many years of assuming a great deal of truth in Martin Luther's

---

10. *New Interpreter's Bible*, 11:179.

assessment that James is an "epistle of straw."[11] Other Reformers did not widely share Luther's distaste.[12]

Some of the pearls or minisermons in the necklace or line that form one sermon about being friends with God are as follows. These minisermons are something like the diatribes in the Greco-Roman culture, yet they are thoroughly religious.

Line of the Text, or Pearls on the Necklace

1. Trials Lead to Perfection

James asks readers to remain steadfast under persecution, which contributes to perfection. Trials develop character and fortitude (1:2–4). In my sense of things, maturity with endurance is close to the meaning of perfection in Matthew: "Be perfect, therefore, as your heavenly Father is perfect" (Matt 5:48). Ask God in prayer and faith for wisdom as your grow, says James (1:5).

2. Tempting Ourselves

Some personal trials come from inordinate desire or disordered passions and not from God. People tempt themselves (1:12–15). Welcome good words that help and save.

3. "Be Doers of the Word"

Doers will be blessed in their doing. The golden clasp that holds these pearls of wisdom together is a very important verse that defines faith in action:

> Religion that is pure and undefiled before God, the Father, is this: to care for orphans and widows in their distress, and to keep oneself unstained by the world. (James 1:27)

Pure religion is a foundation for social action. The clasp of a necklace gives strength and integrity to the string of pearls because a strong clasp holds the necklace together. Service can strengthen personal and communal integrity.

---

11. Harrington, *Who is Jesus?* 160.
12. *New Interpreter's Bible*, 11:177.

4. Practice What You Preach

Do not show partiality to the rich (2:1–13). Financially poor people can be spiritually rich. "Has not God chosen the poor in the world to be rich in faith and to be heirs of the kingdom that he has promised to those who love him?" (2:5). James's words echo Jesus's words in Matthew 5:3 and Luke 6:20 about the poor owning the kingdom. We have to think about how to treat poor people especially well. Loving our neighbor as ourselves is the royal law (2:8). The situation for James's hearers might have been something like the problem addressed in 1 Corinthians, where richer people were at first treated better at the Eucharist or the Lord's Supper.

5. Dead Works

"Faith without works is dead" (2:14–17). James is counterbalancing an exaggerated interpretation of Paul's thought. In Romans 4, Paul stresses that Abraham was reckoned to him as righteousness. An exaggerated interpretation of Romans 4 would be a conclusion that faith does not make moral demands. James points to Abraham's good work in obeying God in order to avoid overstatement about faith. He also cites Rahab, a righteous Gentile who helped the Hebrews. (For an action story with an implicit feminist spin, see Joshua 2:1–24.) Faith means affirmation of monotheism or of belief in one God (James 2:19).

6. Words Matter

Words can both bless and curse (3:9–10). We can use words full of deadly poison to hurt other people who are made in the image of God. We can also use words to bless our Lord and Father. Watch what you say.

7. Sowing Peace

Get rid of bitterness and envy (3:13–14). Selfish ambition is not spiritual wisdom. Real wisdom from above is pure, peaceful and gentle (vv. 16–17). "And a harvest of righteousness is sown in peace for those who make peace" (3:18).

8. Draw Near to God

Turn from worldly envy and draw near to God (4:1–10). If you draw near to God, God will draw near to you. Be friends with God, and God will be a friend with you.

9. Judge Not

Envy can result in slander and sanctimonious judgement of neighbors (4:11–12). This warning about judging others is like wisdom Christ shared in Matthew 7:1: "Do not judge, so that you may not be judged." If we are too hard on others, eventually we will be too hard or unforgiving of ourselves and even afraid to trust in God's forgiveness. Envy can also lead to economic oppression of others. The voices of overworked laborers have reached the ears of the Lord (5:4). Communities should care about sick and suffering people. Be patient, now and in the interim. For examples of suffering, look to the prophets and to Job—a model of patience and endurance (5:10–11). If suffering, pray. If rejoicing, sing (5:14). The prayers of righteous people are effective (5:16). Do not wander from the truth.

The World in Front of the Text
Social Concern and Personal Faith

Consider three reasons to read James. One reason is to find strength for the journey. James can be good spiritual company in the ongoing task of putting faith into practice. Protestants who have been reared in the social gospel tradition and Catholics who embrace liberation theology will find James's convictions to be conducive to their thinking.

Another reason to read James is to find the company of prophets. People who care about social justice are drawn to the Old Testament prophets, who preached God's demand for justice. James's community cared about fairness through caring for orphans and widows in distress (1:27). So it was fitting for the people to look to the prophets. "As an example of suffering and patience, beloved, take the prophets who spoke in the name of the Lord" (5:10).

The prophet Isaiah may have been in the thoughts of people in James's community. Isaiah preached trust in God rather than unholy allegiances. Likewise, James believed that being friends with God and the world at the same time was not possible, at least in his day. Suffering is part of life and can come with belief and practice. The author of James must have known that servants of the Lord could look to Isaiah, who trusted. James could have found hope in the words of his ancestor in faith. "For you shall go out in joy, and be led back in peace; the mountains and the hills before you shall burst into song, and all the trees of the field shall clap their hands" (Is 55:12).

The final reason to read the book of James is to discover core claims about God that support both personal faith and social concern. Three core convictions will resonate with believers in God.

1. God is one (2:19).
2. God cares about the poor (2:5).
3. God listens to prayers of faithful people (1:5–8).

Verbs alone convey a great deal: *Is, Cares, Listens.*

21

The First and Second Letters to Timothy, and the Letter to Titus

Guard the Faith

Overview of 1 Timothy, 2 Timothy, and Titus

First Timothy, 2 Timothy, and Titus are called the *Pastoral Letters* because the authors are concerned about pastoral care, church organization, and preservation of beliefs. These "manifestos" respond to the increased need for organization in church structure and to the threat of competing beliefs.[1]

Paul, or the leader writing in his name, is a pastor to pastors. The author traditionally called Paul tells Timothy and Titus how to be good pastors, pastors who have inner lives that match their external respectability. In addition to setting good examples, these letters summarize beliefs and explain church structure. Organizational strategies in these letters reflect a male-dominated society and particular rather than universal situations.

A developed description of the divine Savior characterizes the Pastoral Letters. God and Christ are equally described as "Savior." There is recognition that Christ functions for God, and that God has acted through Christ. Two faith statements are found in 1 Timothy 2:3–6 and Titus 2:11–14.

First Timothy: Set Your Heart and Hopes on God

Background

What Is 1 Timothy?

First Timothy is a letter that resembles a clergy manual outlining proper behavior for church leaders.

---

1. Duling and Perrin, *New Testament*, 490.

When Was 1 Timothy Written?

The majority of scholars estimate the date of composition as towards the end of the first century AD.[2]

Who Is the Author of 1 Timothy?

Most likely an unknown author who may have had fragments of Paul's writings[3] wrote this letter in Paul's name. He was either a disciple or an editor who understood the issues of the day in light of Paul's thought. Evidence for an author other than Paul includes different vocabulary.[4] The author wrote to Timothy, who was one of Paul's converts, a spiritual child in the faith, and a fellow missionary.

Where Was 1 Timothy Written?

First Timothy was possibly written in Ephesus or, if the author had left there, in Macedonia.[5]

Why Was 1 Timothy Written?

The author does not want any different doctrines taught from the ones Paul had taught (1:3).

Text

Themes and Theological Concerns Shape the Text

Universal in the Particular

The author of 1 Timothy gives specific instructions about clergy deportment and etiquette for all people in the church of his day. Advice, time and place are very particular. However, here are two general concerns that have almost universal implications for Christians and theists of all faiths. The end goal of instruction is "love that comes from a pure heart, a good conscience, and sincere faith" (1:5). The second truth with broad implication is the author's belief that it is better to set one's hopes on God than on "the uncertainty of riches" (6:17).

---

2. Brown, *Introduction to the New Testament*, 654.
3. Ibid., 669, and Harrington, *Who Is Jesus?* 130.
4. Duling and Perrin, *The New Testament*, 486.
5. Brown, *Introduction to the New Testament*, 654.

Pastoral Priorities

Paul's view is that propriety, prayers, and putting pennies into proper perspective matter. People should not be so concerned for wealth that the spiritual life slips out of sight. Timothy is advised to be content with enough because the desire for riches can lead to ruin: "For the love of money is a root of all kinds of evil, and in their eagerness to be rich some have wandered away from the faith and pierced themselves with many pains" (6:10).

Paul as a Herald of Truth

Paul, an apostle, is called a "herald" of gospel truth (2:7). The basic doctrinal differences between the false teachers and the writer of 1 Timothy are not entirely clear. These teachers do forbid marriage and insist on abstinence of certain foods (4:1–5).

Leadership Guidelines

The second-century church had to define leadership roles, draw up job descriptions, and preserve beliefs. The author of 1 Timothy sketches the qualifications of deacons and bishops, who should be temperate, gentle, and respectful (3:2). The bishop must "manage his household," a metaphor for the church (3:4). He should be "well thought of by outsiders" (3:7). In summary, a good bishop is a good manager and is respected in the wider community. Women, referred to in the rules for deacons, may be deacons' wives or deacons (3:8–13). If they were deacons they had strong leadership roles. Women are told to be modest in dress and submissive, and are not to teach men (2:11). "Teaching men" might have meant not bossing husbands around in public. This rule may refer to wealthy women with time on their hands, who were swayed by false teachers and spread the falsehoods.[6]

Prayers and Care

Paul encourages praying for people in high places, and he advises living a quiet life (2:2). Paul tells Timothy how to treat people well. While remaining insistent on the obligation to take care of family, he issues guidelines for widows' groups and stresses care for elderly widows with no means of support (6:17–19). Paul instructs Timothy to guard his ministerial gifts which are the teachings or "what has been entrusted to him" (6:20).

---

6. Ibid., 660–61.

The World in Front of the Text

1. Read 1 Tim 6:10. When people quote this verse they often say, "Money is the root of all evil." Note that the text says "the love of money." What is the difference?

2. The author wrote a provocative metaphor: "By rejecting conscience, certain persons have suffered shipwreck in the faith" (1 Tim 1:19). What could cause you to reject conscience or in some other way to become shipwrecked in faith?

Second Timothy: Be Willing to Share in Suffering and Pursue Righteousness, Faith, Love, and Peace

Background

What Is 2 Timothy?

Second Timothy is a letter.

When Was 2 Timothy Written?

If this letter was written by Paul, the date of composition may be 64 AD. If it was written in Paul's name by a disciple or sympathetic commentator who had fragments of Paul's writings, an estimated date is between 66 and the end of the first century. Even though a disciple probably wrote it, this letter has a better chance of having been authentically Pauline than do the other Pastoral Letters. The letter was probably written in Rome.[7]

Artistic Elements

Focal Point

The focal point is continuity of faith. Paul's cites the faith of Timothy's mother and grandmother (1:5), and he hopes that Timothy will rekindle his inner gift of God (1:6). As you will see in the *Line of Thought*, this letter contains faith statements.

Line of Thought

The author starts his letter with the usual thanksgiving and calls Timothy to "rekindle the gift of God that is within" (1:6). As a herald of truth, Paul

---

7. Brown, *Introduction to the New Testament*, 673.

asks Timothy to "hold to the standard of sound teaching" (1:13). The author chronicles basic beliefs. The main ideas in this first statement of faith are that God saved us and called us with a holy calling, not according to our works but according to grace, which was given to us in Christ Jesus (1:9). This statement of salvation by grace and faith is at the heart of Paul's teaching. A summary of the gospel is found in even shorter form in 2 Timothy chapter 2, verse 8: "Remember Jesus Christ, raised from the dead, a descendent of David—that is my gospel." Verses 11–13 are another faith statement in poetry form. "The saying is sure: If we have died with him, we will also live with him; if we endure, we will also reign with him; if we deny him, he will also deny us; if we are faithless, he remains faithful—for he cannot deny himself." Christ's nature is to be faithful; Christ has to be who he is.

Timothy is encouraged to "be strong in the grace that is in Christ Jesus. Share in suffering like a good soldier of Christ" (2:3). "Shun youthful passions and pursue righteousness, faith, love, and peace, along with those who call on the Lord with a pure heart" (2:22). Paul goes on to urge Timothy to avoid senseless controversies and quarrels, to be kind to everyone, and to correct opponents with gentleness (2:24–25). He points out the vices of the opponents, who love themselves, money, and outward forms of godliness, and says that all Scripture is inspired (3:15–16). Paul urges Timothy to "proclaim the message; be persistent whether the time is favorable or unfavorable; convince, rebuke, and encourage with the utmost patience in teachings"(4:2).

In the style of a farewell message, Paul said that he had been "poured out as a libation" (4:6), that means like a poured drink offering at an Old Testament altar offering or, in the ancient world, a drink offered to God before a sea journey. Making his final confession of faith he said:

> As for me, I am already being poured out as a libation, and the time of my departure has come. I have fought the good fight, I have finished the race, I have kept the faith. From now on there is reserved for me the crown of righteousness, which the Lord, the righteous judge, will give me on that day, and not only to me but also to all who have longed for his appearing. (2 Tim 4:6–8)

The World in Front of the Text

In 2 Tim 3:16, having the Old Testament in mind, Paul states that God inspires all Scripture, and that Scripture is "useful for teaching." Paul stresses the usefulness of Scripture in teaching. This verse raises the question of how to view the concept of inspiration. People who believe that God dictated every word to the biblical authors have stopped reading this book a long time ago. Can you trust the process of remembering the oral traditions, collecting, writing, editing, and selecting material that went into the Bible, without believing that God took away human effort to express in words? Could God have breathed into human beings the motivation to present the truth as clearly as possible?

Titus: In the Present Age, Live Godly Lives for the Sake of the Faith

Background

What Is Titus?

Titus is a letter.

When Was Titus Written?

If Titus was written in the name of Paul, as most scholars believe, then it was written at the end of the first century AD or at the start of the second century AD.[8]

By Whom Was Titus Written?

Probably a disciple of Paul or a very understanding commentator wrote this letter to Titus in Crete. We will call the author Paul on the theory that if Paul did have a letter-writing ministry late in life, then these books the Pastoral Letters are what he would have written.

Where Was Titus Written?

Ephesus may be the place of composition.

Why was Titus written?

Paul wrote this letter "for the sake of the faith" (1:1) In short, his concerns were sound doctrine and steadfastness.

---

8. Ibid., 639.

Texture and Text

In the salutation, Paul appropriates the Old Testament concept of servant and applies it to himself (see 2 Sam 7:5 and Jer 7:25). The concept of Christians as "God's elect" is based on Isa 65:9: "I will bring forth descendents from Jacob, and from Judah inheritors of my mountains; my chosen shall inherit it, and my servants shall settle there." Thus the understanding of the servant nature of leadership has a richly textured history. The letter of Titus starts by describing Paul as a servant of God and an apostle to proclaim the faith of the church.

Titus is told to appoint elders (1:5), who were a lot like boards of trustees in churches today. Qualities that bishops, as God's stewards, should have are not being arrogant or quick tempered and, in a positive vein, being "devout" and hospitable (1:7–8). The most serious accusation against false teachers is that "they deny [God] by their actions" (1:16). Titus was told to preach sound doctrine. Older men are to be "temperate," "prudent," and "sound in faith" (2:1–2). Women are told to be submissive in the spirit of the social constraints of the day and thus to commend the Christian message (2:5). Elders, including Titus, are to be "models of good works" and are to "urge younger men to be self-controlled" (2:6–7). Paul spoke of Jesus saying, "He it is who gave himself for us that he might redeem us from all iniquity and purify for himself a people of his own who are zealous for good deeds" (2:14).

The author honors the Pauline heritage and stresses Paul's conviction of justification by faith rather than by works. His summary statement was associated with baptism (3:5):

> But when the goodness and loving kindness of God our Savior appeared, he saved us, not because of any works of righteousness that we had done, but according to his mercy, through the water of rebirth and renewal by the Holy Spirit. (Titus 3:4–5)

Response to the loving kindness of God and acceptance of Christ are such powerful actions that baptism was understood as birth and as a turning point in life. Avoid stupid controversies. Good works meet urgent needs and keep people productive (3:5–8). The concluding benediction is "Grace be with all of you" (3:15).

The World in Front of the Text

Are there gold nuggets in the muck and mire of doctrine and debate? Yes. In college, one of my religion professors, Lawrence Meredith, often said that taking the Lord's name in vain is not saying "damn it" or worse, but saying that you believe in God and acting as if you do not. He did not quote chapter and verse, yet clearly his biblical source is Titus 1:16. where the author criticizes his opponents for professing to know God but denying him by their actions.

The false teachers are not the only people in the history of the world to deny God by their actions. We all do that sometimes. Think about it. If you wish, write a letter or prayer to God explaining how you have denied him by your actions or thoughts. Offering your thoughts and feelings to God is being a loyal child in the faith. To put it a different way if you are not a theist, do you ever get in the way of love at work in the world?

Part Six

Christians in Crisis

22

The First Letter of Peter

If Persecuted, Be Culturally Conservative and Confidently Cast Cares upon God

Overview of the Community of 1 Peter and Continuing Consolation for Christians

BY WRITING to a community that was not comfortable in the general culture, the author fashioned his deed to the future. The first readers felt like aliens. Feeling like strangers may have been symbolic rather than literal, or, on the other hand, they may have experienced persecution under Nero, or local persecution under Domitian.[1] The people of the community of 1 Peter may have been like migrant workers who were on the margins of society, or they may have been alienated from the world at large because of their beliefs. In any case, prospects of social or political persecution were in the air, and Peter's people did not feel at home in the world.

The Christians that Peter addresses were alienated and looked down upon because they were different religiously and ethically. If Roman officials were actively persecuting the Christians, the author would not likely have urged them to honor the emperor. At the same time, they had no choice but to work within their social situation.

The writer of 1 Peter guides his community, and also future readers, towards a blessed spiritual life. Three dimensions of this letter that are helpful in finding joy despite suffering are theological convictions, spiritual hopes, and practical ethical advice.

---

1. Duling and Perrin, *New Testament*, 476.

Theological Convictions

Three theological convictions are:

1. Through the resurrection of Jesus we have new birth into a living hope (1:3).
2. Faith like gold is refined by fire (1:7)
3. Belief leads to rejoicing with glorious joy (1:8).

Spiritual Hopes

The potential of unbelievers is cause for hope. Honorable conduct may lead pagan people to eventually glorify God. Believing wives might convert their partners (3:1–2).

Ethical Advice

As off-putting as the household codes may be today, these codes suggest that convention may reduce stress in the family, especially when outside cultural pressures are difficult. Classic ethical advice for church people is found in the instructions to get rid of malice (2:1) and to serve one another with one's gifts (4:10). A church where people get along is more enjoyable than a church divided. If a person wonders if the world is ultimately friendly, small church groups can nurture trust in God's good will. God's household must have been a safe haven of happiness for Peter's people. Today small classes and other friendly, support groups offer safe places for people to share their thoughts and feelings, which sometimes are at odds with the prevailing culture.

Background

What Is 1 Peter?

First Peter is a sermonlike general letter to a cluster of churches, a letter that was written in the name of Peter.[2] Within the letter there are household codes, hymn fragments, and allusions to sayings from the Sermon on the Mount, perhaps from sources earlier than the Gospels. A few scholars have suggested that this letter could include a reworked baptismal homily.[3] That possibility at least points to the importance of baptism for the community.

---

2. Harrington, *Who Is Jesus?* 164–65.
3. Ibid., 165, and Duling and Perrin, *New Testament*, 475.

The First Letter of Peter

The content of 1 Peter is not only about the way to live Christian lives, but also how to survive in a cold, critical climate. First Peter encourages cultural conservatism and at the same time cultural critique. People are called to high ethical standards in order to live holy lives and be witnesses of virtue to a pagan world.

When Was 1 Peter Written?

If written in Peter's name, this book was likely written between AD 80 and 90.[4]

By Whom Was 1 Peter Written?

Although Peter as an elderly man might have dictated this letter to his secretary, a disciple of Peter carrying on the heritage of Peter is a more likely candidate for authorship.[5] As Duling and Perrin point out, the writer had traditions about Jesus but did not attribute the sayings to Jesus. It seems highly unlikely that Jesus's leading disciple, the Peter of the Gospels, would not quote Jesus directly.[6]

The author, whom we will call Peter, is a combined coach and cheerleader. He wrote to Christians, most of whom were not Jews first.[7]

Where Was 1 Peter Written?

Most likely this letter was written in Rome. The code name for Rome is Babylon and is mentioned in 5:13.

Why Was 1 Peter Written?

Peter wrote to give Christians strength to live in a hostile environment and to address their suffering through looking for meaning in the example of Jesus. In the author's view, suffering tests faith (1:7). It is better to suffer for doing right and following God's will than for doing wrong (3:17). Christ was righteous and "put to death in the flesh" but "made alive in the spirit" (3:18). Christ is our example of suffering because "he did not return abuse" but "entrusted himself to the one who judges justly" (2:23). Because the faithful have come to trust God through Jesus, they can, even

---

4. Ibid., 165.
5. Brown, *Introduction to the New Testament*, 706.
6. Duling and Perrin, *New Testament*, 474.
7. Harrington, *Who Is Jesus?* 167.

when harassed, entrust themselves to a faithful Creator while continuing to do good deeds (4:19).

Text

In this letter, living hope flows into formation of Christian identity and on to witness in a pagan world and finally to ethical behavior under persecution. Stages of Christian maturity are identity, witness, and ethics. After the greeting, Peter blesses God and summarizes the belief of faith. "Blessed be the God and Father of our Lord Jesus Christ! By his great mercy he has given us a new birth into a living hope through the resurrection of Jesus Christ from the dead" (1:3).

Identity

In chapter 1, Peter addresses the exiled people. His statement of faith and identity is that his people have been given "a new birth into a living hope through the resurrection of Jesus Christ from the dead" (1:3). Quoting the Old Testament book of Leviticus, the author reminds his readers that God is holy and calls us to be holy. There is a hint of universalism here, with generous goodwill towards the oppressors, who are not completely written off as having no potential for goodness: "If you invoke as Father the one who judges all people impartially according to their deeds, live in reverent fear during the time of your exile" (1:17). The author does not want the community to go backwards to a former life that was less pure and holy. He stresses that God gave new birth and living hope through the resurrection of Jesus. A good memory verse is 1 Peter 1:21: "Through him you have come to trust in God, who raised him from the dead and gave him glory, so that your faith and hope are set on God."

Witness

In chapter 2, readers are directed to "rid yourself of malice, insincerity and slander" (v. 1). God's people are called to be like living stones built into a spiritual house, a holy people (v. 5). Christ is the cornerstone of God's people (v. 6). Peter reminds his readers—in a little poem with an enormous theological message inserted into the narrative—that they are now God's people who have received mercy: "Once you were not a people, but now you are God's people; once you had not received mercy, but now you have received mercy" (v. 10). At this point, non-Christians were sometimes called "Gentiles": "Conduct yourselves honorably among the Gentiles, so that, though they malign you as evildoers, they may see your honorable deeds and glorify God when he comes to judge" (v. 12). In other words, behave well so that outsiders in the pagan world will see your honorable deeds and eventually glorify God. For the Lord's sake accept the authority of institutions. Live as free people, but do not abuse freedom. Honor everyone. Honor the emperor (v. 17). Christ is our example because he did not return abuse when he suffered (vv. 21–23).

Ethics

In 1 Peter chapter 3, wives are to "accept the authority of your husbands" (v. 1). (However, wives are not asked to accept the pagan religion of unbelieving husbands.) Husbands should be considerate (v. 7). Speaking in the spirit of Jesus, Peter says:

> Finally, all of you, have unity of spirit, sympathy, love for one another, a tender heart, and a humble mind. Do not repay evil for evil or abuse for abuse; but, on the contrary, repay with a blessing. (vv. 8–9)

(Blessing is protection from destructive malice. However, pastors and teachers need to stress that responding to abuse with a blessing does not sanction domestic violence.)

In the hymn that follows (3:10–12), the phrase "seek peace and pursue it" (3:11) deserves pondering. Sometimes getting along with others is a matter of wanting to relate without strife. If you suffer for doing right, you are blessed. Jesus was killed in body but "made alive in the spirit" (3:18). Remembering good Noah and unity in baptism helped the people strive with good consciences toward holiness (3:20–22).

In chapter 4, community members are called to better behavior—even if they are harassed—than was customary in wider society. Do not be drunk or carousing (4:3). Be hospitable and share your gifts as good stewards (4:7–9). Stress from the threat of persecution may have undermined love for one another in community and marriages. If so, the author addressed that problem saying, "Above all, maintain constant love for one another, for love covers a multitude of sins" (4:8). If you are reviled for Christ, you are blessed. (This thought echoes the beatitudes in Matthew, especially Matt 5:10.) In suffering, entrust yourself to God, our Creator. Continue to do the good.

In chapter 5, church leaders should tend their flocks like the Chief Shepherd (5:4), who is Christ. Cast you cares upon God (5:7). Christ will restore, support, and strengthen you (5:10).

Part Six: Christians in Crisis

The World in Front of the Text

Many Christians fit quite comfortably into American society. However, every Christian has to decide how to relate to culture. Is there anything in our society that you question? Some areas to consider are use of television; sexuality; spending, saving, or giving money; the commercialization of Christmas; and war.

23

The Letter of Jude

Freedom in Christ Does Not Mean
Exemption from Moral Authority

Background

JUDE IS a very short, opinionated letter. No one knows for sure when Jude was written. Estimated dates range from AD 50 to 100.[1] The brothers of Jesus were popular and respected preachers, so this letter probably was written from Palestine where the brothers were remembered and respected. Either Jesus's youngest brother or a younger spiritual brother of Jesus wrote Jude. If Jude the youngest brother of Jesus wrote this letter, it had to have been written nearer 50 AD than 100. If he did not author the letter, the date would be nearer to AD 100. In any case, writing this book was a supportive, brotherly task. Brotherly Jude writes this letter "to those who are called, who are beloved by God and kept safe for Jesus Christ" (v. 1).

Jude writes with pastoral concern to point out the dangers of teachers who taught that the grace of God freed them to do as they pleased in many ways that made the community less pure and holy. His short letter warns against departure from the teachings of the church and denounces leaders who tempt people away from belief. (We do not have those leaders' side of the story.) The warning (vv. 17–23) is that it is important to base one's life on the faith, or else one will be "devoid of the Spirit" (v. 19), just as the opponents are. In summary, "keep yourself in the love of God" (v. 21). Jude stresses that good behavior is consistent with faith, and that bad behavior is a perversion of gospel and grace.

Texture helps the writer make his points. Texture comes from the richness of varied images and allusions to other biblical passages. Jude

---

1. Brown, *Introduction to the New Testament*, 749.

uses several images to describe the teachers who taught that freedom in Christ meant moral exemption. He says that they are "waterless clouds"; "uprooted trees without fruit"; "wandering stars"; and "wild waves of the sea, casting up the foam of their own shame" (vv. 12–13). Fruit is a common biblical metaphor for righteous living, so fruitlessness is not good. Waterless clouds reflect Proverbs 25:14: "Like clouds and wind without rain is one who boasts of a gift never given."

Jude looks through the lens of Christian responsibility to abide by Christian traditions. To reiterate, his perspective is that turning into licentiousness God's freely offered grace in Jesus means disowning Jesus. In contrast to abandoning Jesus, "the positive ideal of Christian life is expressed in a trinitarian formula: 'pray in the Holy Spirit; keep yourselves in the love of God; look forward to the mercy of our Lord Jesus Christ that leads to eternal life'" (v. 21).[2]

Text

The line of thought in Jude is that the faithful need to "contend for the faith" (v. 3) by making sure that new life in Christ is not perverted into doing anything regardless of consequences. Jude shows that behavior has consequences by referring to individuals and situations from Old Testament times. People in Jude's community who were blemishes on the love feast were concerned only for themselves and turned the feast into a big party (v. 12). If you were the biological or spiritual brother or sister of Jesus, and people were misrepresenting Jesus's teachings, would you not be angry?

The letter-speech concludes with a doxology that includes the first line of a benediction used in some churches: "Now to him who is able to keep you from falling" (v. 24). In this doxology, God is the keeper.

The World in Front of the Text

Practice Discernment

Consider the phrase "wild waves of the sea, casting up the foam of their own shame" (v. 13). Is destructive behavior such as "road rage" or speech that totally disregards the feelings and rights of others and that results in a metaphorical frothing of the mouth, a form of environmental or community pollution? Is freedom of expression ever a perversion of Christian freedom? Is lawless behavior ever a result of shame or the result of a sense of being nobody without anything to lose by hurtful behavior?

---

2. Harrington, *Who Is Jesus?* 172.

Reflect on a Painting

The artist Samuel Palmer (1805–1881) liked William Blake and his mystical art. Palmer was also drawn to medieval art, and his luminous colors are reminiscent of illuminated manuscripts. You can find his painting in Sister Wendy's *The Story of Painting*.[3]

Palmer's painting *Coming from Evening Church* evokes two interrelated phrases in Jude. These phrases are "kept safe for Jesus Christ" (v. 1) and "keep yourself in the love of God" (v. 21). In Palmer's picture, a community of faithful people leave church after the evening service. They have done their part to keep themselves in the love of God. Two trees bend inward to form a shape like an arched church window frame, as if nature and God gently hold the community safely together for Jesus. When nature and grace converge, *beauty* is the word.

---

3. Beckett, *Story of Painting*, 27.

24

The Second Letter of Peter

Wait Patiently for New Heavens and a New Earth, Where Righteousness Is at Home

Background

An Expansion of Jude

Second Peter is a homily or meditation in the form of a letter, and an expansion upon Jude, which is quoted but not acknowledged as a source.[1] A likely date for 2 Peter is AD 130, give or take a decade.[2] Most of Jude is part of 2 Peter. Like Jude, 2 Peter stresses apostolic or inherited faith understood as a body of teachings. Virtues in 2 Peter build upon Jude's idea of being "kept safe for Jesus" (Jude 1). In 2 Peter, Christian virtues are ways of responding to God's grace.[3] Many scholars regard 2 Peter as the latest book in the New Testament.[4]

Written in the Name and Spirit of Peter

The author of 2 Peter was not the same person as the author of 1 Peter, yet the writer of the later book followed the accepted literary practice of writing a testament and final message for another person. He wrote to a general audience in the eastern Mediterranean area that knew Paul's writings and 1 Peter. Second Peter might have been written from Rome.[5]

---

1. Brown, *Introduction to the New Testament*, 761.
2. Ibid., 762.
3. Harrington, *Who Is Jesus?* 177.
4. Ibid., 177.
5. Brown, *Introduction to the New Testament*, 762.

The Second Letter of Peter

Assurance and Guidance

The author of 2 Peter wanted people to know that just because Jesus had not returned did not mean that Jesus would never return. Second Peter's author sees the transfiguration of Jesus (2 Pet 1:17–18; see also Mark 9:2–8) as anticipation of the full glory of the risen Christ and confirmation that Christ will come again.[6] Meanwhile, with a hopeful attitude, the author offers the possibility of becoming "participants in the divine nature" (1:4) by supporting faith "with goodness, and goodness with knowledge, and knowledge with self-control, and self-control with endurance, and endurance with godliness, and godliness with mutual affection, and mutual affection with love" (1:5–7).

Text

After the opening address, that is, the salutation, the author discusses the calling to Christian living. As a spiritual cheerleader, he assures his readers that they can participate in the divine nature (1:3). He wants people to escape the corruption that is in the world. While affirming gifts of grace and power to live a godly life, the author stresses the necessity of keeping up the good work of having self-control, faith, perseverance, and love for one another (1:5–7). Confirming our callings through Christian living is "entry into the eternal kingdom of our Lord and Savior Jesus Christ" (1:11). The author recalls Jesus's transfiguration in Mark's gospel. He envisions the second coming to be something like the transfiguration. Thus the author imagines Christ's returning based on experiences in the past. Writing as Peter would have spoken, the author advises attentiveness and hopefulness until "the day dawns and the morning star rises in your hearts" (1:19). This metaphor is very gentle, in contrast to the metaphor or fire in 3:10. If both are understood as purifying, the main implication is renewal. In 2 Peter chapter 2, Noah is portrayed as a herald of righteousness (v. 4) who points to assurance that the Lord rescues the godly (v. 9).

Opponents of Peter are blemishes because they turn the church's fellowship into a sham. Sin is "hearts trained in greed" (2:14) and slavery to corruption or to whatever masters people (2:19). In chapter 3, verse 4, the author scoffs at those who do not believe in the second coming of Christ. His opponents might have advocated a realized eschatology and present salvation that permitted libertine practice.[7]

---

6. Harrington, *Who Is Jesus?* 175.
7. Brown, *Introduction to the New Testament*, 765.

Be Patient

Drawing upon Psalm 90, the author of 2 Peter finds perspective and affirms that in the eyes of the Lord, a thousand years is a day (3:8). He says, "we wait for new heavens and a new earth, where righteousness is at home" (3:13). Meanwhile, strive to be peaceful and pure (3:14), and "grow in the grace and knowledge of our Lord and Savior Jesus Christ" (3:18).

The World in Front of the Text
Thinking About Communal Interpretations

1. Second Peter speaks of a received faith in chapter 1, verse 1. Also, in chapter 1, verse 20, the author contends that no prophecy of Scripture is a matter of one's own interpretation. How do you understand these verses within your tradition?

   A. If you belong to a church that stresses your right to interpret the Bible for yourself, do you think it is ever possible to read the Bible without the beliefs of your church affecting your understanding?

   B. If you belong to a church that stresses the importance of the church's teachings about Scripture, can you ever disagree with official teachings?

2. What is your vision of the world where righteousness is at home? Do the virtues in 2 Peter 1:5–7 inform your hopes? Whether or not you believe in a literal second coming, can you imagine a time when peace, forgiveness, and love of neighbor rule in people's hearts?

Thinking about Personal Interpretation and Artistic Exploration

"The dawn of a new day with the morning star rising within your hearts" (2 Pet 1:19) is an evocative metaphor. In historical context, the "rising star" referred to the return of Christ. To individualize this image, whenever the love of Christ rises within you, there is a little earthly second coming. Imagine a star rising in a dark sky that has just started to turn from navy to morning-glory blue. Perhaps you could paint a picture or write a poem about a time when you felt compassionate towards people, or hopeful about the future of the world.

Part Seven

Jesus as Helper, and Christ as Risen Lord

25

The Letter to the Hebrews
Reflect on Christ the High Priest, and Continue in Faithfulness

Overview
Jesus as Helper for Tired Christians

The author of Hebrews pondered and proclaimed the importance and meanings of Jesus for second-generation Christians, who were very tired. His finer theological points about Christ and the background of his writing will make more sense after considering the pastoral needs of his first audience.

As the author-preacher Mr. Philosopher saw it, the main problems facing second-generation Christians were departure from tradition (Heb 2:1) and sluggishness (6:12). The author's main plea was "do not abandon confidence (10:35). Yet, in light of their spiritual and emotional struggles, his community was growing tired, and weariness undermines confidence. Recalling the history of endurance could help: "But recall those earlier day when, after you had been enlightened, you endured a hard struggle with sufferings, sometimes being publicly exposed to abuse and persecution" (10:32–33).

Second-generation Christians lived in a shame-based society. Thus, ridicule and rejection were torturous. While bloodshed had not generally come to pass, it appeared to be a threat (12:4).[1] Like ancestors before them, they felt like aliens and were not comfortable in their culture. The author offered four hopeful positions that could help Christians in his time carry on with faith and trust:

---

1. *New Interpreter's Bible*, 12:9.

1. Freedom from the fear of death: Since Jesus shared in the human condition that includes death and was raised, he destroyed the power of death, to "free those who were held in slavery by the fear of death" (Heb 2:15). In the author's view, salvation involves liberation from the fear of death (2:13–15) and rest in God (4:11). A heavenly country (11:16) suggests ongoing life in Christ beyond earthly life and worship.

2. Heavenly help: The author had a theological understanding about God's accessibility and presence. Because Christians have a high priest, in Jesus, who knew what it is like to be a human being, they are able to boldly "approach the throne of grace" and find mercy and grace in time of need (4:14–16). According to the writer of Hebrews, the risen Christ holds his priesthood permanently and lives forever to make intercession for those who approach him (7:22–25).

3. Connection with spiritual ancestors: Ancestors had gone through the same kinds of trouble and endured with faith even though they were strangers and foreigners on the earth (11:13–14). Thus, there was continuity and connection with ancestors of faithfulness.

4. A Trustworthy God: These early Christians found, and people of faith today can find, assurance that God keeps his promises. The author conveys God's trustworthy nature by reminding his audience that Abraham knew that Sarah would conceive as God said because Abraham considered "him faithful who had promised" (11:11).

Background

What Is Hebrews, and When Was It Written?

Hebrews is a philosophic sermon or homily with an ending that is like a notation that the author stuck on at the last minute. This sticky note states, "word of exhortation" (13:22–25). Although he may have followed a literary convention of his time, the author might have labeled the form of his writing after it was complete, and when he saw what he had done. The elegant sermon is also a Christian exploration of the Old Testament. An estimated date between AD 60 and 95 may be the "chronological frame."[2]

---

2. *New Interpreter's Bible*, 12:8.

The Author and His Place

The author and place of composition are not known with certainty. "The Church Father Origen said that only God knows who wrote Hebrews."[3] However, we do know some things about the author. He lived and worked within the apostolic tradition of what had been heard and taught. He understood Judaism, wrote superb Greek, and knew some Greek philosophy and the techniques of Greek rhetoric or speech making. He used the Greek translation of the Old Testament known as the Septuagint, which informed his thought process. The author also drew upon Platonic thought and Hellenistic Judaism.[4] In summary, Fred B. Craddock, writing in the *New Interpreter's Bible*, says that if the readers were Hellenistic Jewish Christians, a good guess is that there were in Rome.[5]

Why Was Hebrews Written?

The writer wanted to help second-generation Christians to remain faithful and confident. He wrote, "Do not, therefore, abandon that confidence of yours; it brings a great reward" (10:35). His main definition of sin was transgression from God's will. A hymn title, "Trust and Obey," captures the author's desires for his readers' spiritual lives.

Artistic Features

Focal Point

The belief that the risen Christ is a high priest is the focal point of the sermon. The author says that the main point is that we have a high priest, who is seated at the right hand of the Majesty, or God, in heaven (8:1). I used to think that Hebrews chapter 11, often called the *faith chapter*, is the most important. Yet, belief that we have a high priest who lives to make intercession can help people sustain faith.

Distillation of Ethics

Ethics flow from the focal point. When nourished by confidence that there is divine intercession or transcendent help, people want to please God. In Hebrews three things are especially pleasing to God. They are faith (11:5–6), worship with reverence and awe (12:28), and sharing

---

3. Harrington, *Who Is Jesus?* 141.
4. *New Interpreter's Bible*, 12:7.
5. Ibid., 12:10.

(13:16). The author's distillation of what pleases God suggests practices in Christianity and other religions. Reverence for life, sharing, and faith that ultimately the universe is friendly can be personal qualities or both theists and nontheists.

Counterbalance

It seems to me that clearly the author stresses the superiority of Christ over Moses. In his time, it must have been important to stress the superiority of the Christ and to emphasize spiritual sacrifice and worship in the inner temple of the heart, so that the faithful would not be tempted to go back to religions protected by the state. However, it also seems to me that the author's attitude is counterbalanced with high regard for continuity with people of faith in the Old Testament.

Perspective

With his pilgrim feet on solid ground, the author sets his poet's eyes on the vanishing point, the farthest spot on land or sea that reaches and touches eternity. His long-distance vision is 20/20. In the author's sightings true perspective is gained by aligning ourselves to eternity. To his mind, when persecution results in a crisis of confidence, the best answer is a more complete Christology, that is, a more complete understanding of Christ.

He stresses that Jesus was a human being; yet as the risen Christ at God's right hand, Jesus is a heavenly high priest (8:1–2). In a spirit of applause (like "Encore, encore!"), the writer cites the faith of spiritual ancestors (11:1–40). Jesus is our model or "the pioneer and perfecter of faith" (12:1–2).

Words That Color the Writing

The theologian-author used well-thought-through words.

God

The author is not so concerned with Jesus that he forgets about God. The most important characteristic of God in Hebrews is that God speaks: God speaks through the prophets (1:1); God speaks through a Son (1:2); God speaks through the Old Testament (4:7; 7:21; 8:8–12); God speaks through the Holy Spirit (10:15–17).

New Covenant

In chapter 8 the author outright calls "obsolete" the old covenant based on Hebrew law (v. 13). Whether *obsolete* has to mean "invalid" is another matter. Remember *new* in the biblical sense can mean "updated" or "renewed." In any case, Christ is the mediator of a new covenant, which is beautifully described in chapter 8. If you wish read this chapter. Verse 10b says a lot: "I will put my laws in their minds, and write them on their hearts, and I will be their God, and they shall be my people."

High priest

Hebrews is about Christ the eternal high priest. The understanding of Christ as high priest is developed in chapters 5–10. Jesus the high priest willingly offered his life as sacrifice for sins. Thus, he is both the sacrifice, and the priest who made the sacrifice. Christ was self-giving. According to Hebrews 7:25, Christ lives to make intercession. Paul, in Romans 8:26, where he says that the "Spirit intercedes with sighs too deep for words," supports the author of Hebrews. The concept of the priesthood of Christ in Hebrews is about understanding Jesus's death on the cross rather than directly about the ministerial priesthood of all believers.

Once for all

Hebrews chapter 10 contains a description of Christ as a once and for all sacrifice (10:10) As Lawrence Meredith pointed out during my college days, the main implication of Christ's sacrifice on the cross is that no more animal sacrifices are necessary. Putting an end to animal ritual sacrifices opened the way for worship as sacrifice of praise and offering of good deeds (Heb 10:24; 13:15).

Faith

If you can only read a little of Hebrews, please read chapter 11. A good memory verse is chapter 11, verse 1: "Now faith is the assurance of things hoped for, the conviction of things not seen." The author applauds the good examples of people of faith from the Old Testament. Abraham had faith, as did Moses and his parents, who hid Moses in the bulrushes when he was a baby. These faithful people point to Jesus as model. Then, in chapter 12 the author of Hebrews pictures Jesus as the "pioneer . . . of our faith," who endured hostility and death. The author used the athletic image of a race and urges Christians to endure: "Let us run with perseverance the race that is set before us, looking to Jesus the pioneer and perfecter of our faith" (12:1–2).

Second coming

The author affirms the second coming of Christ. In the meantime, a guiding ethical principle is that Christians should be hospitable to strangers and in so doing may have "entertained angels without knowing it" (13:2). Visiting people in prison (13:3–4) and remaining chaste in marriage are also virtuous parts of the Christian life. The author advises being content with modest wealth (3:5) and trusting that God will not leave or forsake us. Drawing upon Psalm 118, the author says, "The Lord is my helper; I will not be afraid. What can anyone do to me?" (13:6). The author's faith converges with Paul's in Romans 8 where Paul says that nothing can separate us from the love of God (Rom 8:39).

Text

As a sermon, Hebrews has three parts, with three main points:

- Part I (chapters 1–4): Jesus as God's word is superior to angels and Moses.
- Part II (chapters 5–10): Jesus is the great high priest.
- Part III (chapters 11–13): Jesus is a model of faith.

Part 1

Chapter 1   In days past, God spoke through prophets. In Christ, God spoke through a son. Christ is the reflection and exact imprint of God (1:3). The Son is superior to angels (1:5–9).

Chapter 2   Jesus is the pioneer of salvation. He became perfect or mature through suffering and therefore is trustworthy. He became like us, so he understands the human condition: "Therefore he had to become like his brothers and sisters in every respect, so that he might be a merciful and faithful high priest in the service of God, to make a sacrifice of atonement for the sins of the people" (2:17–18). Jesus is our brother and can understand temptation and be merciful in his work as priest.

Chapter 3   Jesus is superior to Moses (3:3). Moses was faithful as a servant. Jesus is faithful as a son.

Chapter 4   God promises heavenly rest that believers realize in part on earth: "So then, a sabbath rest still remains for the people of God; for those who enter God's rest also cease from their labors as God did from his" (4:9–10).

Part 2

Chapter 5   Jesus is the great high priest appointed by God.

Chapter 6   Jesus was a forerunner on our behalf.

Chapter 7   Jesus was not a priest through biological lineage. The author reasons that Christ's priesthood is eternal because he was a priest according to the order of Melchizedek. Because the Scriptures are silent about Melchizedek's ancestors, the author of Hebrews infers that he did not have any and was thus eternal.

Chapter 8   In Jesus we have a heavenly high priest.

Chapter 9   Jesus as high priest can be a mediator for us in the presence of God.

Chapter 10 Christ's sacrifice was "once for all" (10:10). Believers can approach God in a full assurance of faith, and forgiveness holding fast to conviction and helping others to love and do good deeds.

Part 3

Chapter 11 This chapter is sometimes called "the faith chapter." It is probably the best-known chapter in Hebrews. "Now faith is the assurance of things hoped for, the conviction of things not seen. Indeed, by faith our ancestors received approval" (11:1–2). Faith was the power through which the Old Testament heroes did their work. Time after time, Old Testament models—Abel, Enoch, Noah, Abraham, and Moses—showed faith.

Chapter 12 "So great a cloud of witnesses" surrounds us (12:1). Jesus's witness was to endure the cross for the joy ahead. Jesus was faithful in suffering and is our example of faith and perseverance. Created things can be shaken, but the kingdom cannot be shaken (12:27). Acceptable worship entails reverence and awe: "Therefore, since we are receiving a kingdom that cannot be shaken, let us give thanks, by which we offer to God

Chapter 13   an acceptable worship with reverence and awe; for indeed our God is a consuming fire" (12:28–29).

Chapter 13   "Let mutual love continue. Do not neglect to show hospitality to strangers, for by doing that some have entertained angels without knowing it" (13:1–2). We can know with confidence that God is our helper. Quoting Psalm 118:6, the author declares: "'The Lord is my helper; I will not be afraid. What can anyone do to me?'" (13:6).

Like preachers in many worship assemblies, the author of Hebrews concludes the sermon part of the letter with a benediction:

> Now may the God of peace, who brought back from the dead our Lord Jesus, the great shepherd of the sheep, by the blood of the eternal covenant, make you complete in everything good so that you may do his will, working among us that which is pleasing in his sight, through Jesus Christ, to whom be the glory forever and ever. Amen. (13:20–21)

An Image of Christ in the Foreground

Christ cannot be completely portrayed by any verbal or pictorial image. However one portrait of *Christ* that was in a former church named Hagia Sophia that is now a museum in Istanbul captures the spirit of Christ the intercessor and high priest in Hebrews. The gold background suggests majesty in this image of Christ as the *Pantocrator* or "divine ruler of the universe." Christ looks wise, as if he could say exactly the right penetrating word (see Heb 4:12). In Christian art, the image of Jesus as the Good Shepherd evolved into Christ the Ruler of All, the *Pantocrator*. Yet at the same time, this thirteenth-century work also retains a gentle, human spirit in Jesus, who as depicted in Hebrew was like us in earthly life and thus able to understand the human condition as well as being an eternal, unchangeable priest in a heavenly realm. In Hebrews, Christ the ruler and great shepherd (13:20) has nurturing qualities like the Lord, the good shepherd in Psalm 23. You can find this picture of Christ the *Pantocrator* in many art history books, including in the classic *History of Art* by H.W. Janson.[6]

---

6. Janson, *History of Art*, 199.

26

The Book of Revelation

Endure with Faith, and Know That in the End God Will Wipe Away Every Tear

Background

What Is Revelation?

REVELATION IS a very difficult book. This letter, which is a mixture of different forms of writing, is more like art and poetry than an essay expounding ideas. Like other New Testament letters it has a salutation, opening benediction, body, and closing benediction. Because seven churches receive individualized messages, the hint is that Revelation was passed from church to church. More important, Revelation is an apocalypse and conversely an apocalypse is a revelation. Often an apocalyptic story is a narrative in which a person who is in a very difficult situation receives a vivid vision of future help. When evil is so pervasive that a situation within history seems impossible, yearnings for vindication beyond earthly time may invite revelatory insights. Most important, Revelation is a work of Christian imagination that celebrates the risen Christ. Yet this book is also prophetic literature because John of Patmos was a prophet as well as a visionary. In Revelation 10:11 he is told he must prophesy against people, nations, and kings. John places himself in the category of prophet (22:9). Prophets are mouthpieces for God and God's justice. They are not primarily forecasters of the future. In the prophetic tradition, Revelation is a prophecy of judgment for the wicked and justice for the righteous.

By Whom Was Revelation Written?

A man named John wrote Revelation to churches in the western sector of Asia Minor. He was an apocalyptic prophet who wrote the most apocalyptic book in the New Testament. Although he shared some themes with

John of the Gospel (themes such as Jesus as living water and as the Lamb), the writer of Revelation was not the John who wrote the Gospel of John;[1] John's gospel is the least apocalyptic book in the New Testament.

John the author of Revelation wrote in exile on the island of Patmos. He was exiled because he preached the gospel message of God's redemptive activity carried through history. His dramatization of the gospel was likely read aloud to the first audience, who wanted the church to survive and grow. John had faith in God's power, deeply internalized belief in Scripture (especially of Daniel 7:2–8) to drawn upon in times of need, emerging insights and motivation to record the revelatory vision he saw while "in the Spirit." The revelation was from Christ and about Christ. This vision is for people of any time or place who are persecuted for their faith and need words of encouragement and hope.

When and Where Was Revelation Written?

The book was written between 92 and 96 AD, at the end of the reign of Emperor Domitian.[2] The small island of Patmos is sixty miles southwest of Ephesus so the letter was likely written in the Ephesus area.

Why Was Revelation Written?

John wanted to encourage oppressed, tired people with transcendent images of victory. Emperor worship, which was forced upon John's people, was against their belief that the only proper worship is of God. John said there was no compromise. The author wrote in chapter 13 verse 10: "Here is a call for endurance and faith of the saints." John needed to address the question, *who really is Lord?* His answer, presented in dramatic images, is that the emperor of Rome is not the Lord. Christ Jesus is sovereign.

Common Mistakes

1. An important thing to note about the title of the book of Revelation is that *Revelation* is not spelled with an *s* on the end. This first mistake (a very common one) is easy to make because there are so many visions in Revelation; it seems at first that *Revelation* should have an *s* on the end. However, the main vision or revelation is that God will win out over evil.

---

1. Brown, *Introduction to the New Testament*, 774.
2. Ibid., 774.

2. The second most likely mistake is to read Revelation as a blueprint for the end of the world. Since the book is concerned with future judgment and the second coming of Christ and the triumph of God, it is understandable that people try to find a code within the text that predicts the end of the world as we know it. This interpretation does not do justice to the historical situation. It is best to read Revelation as an imaginative work that celebrates the risen Christ and tells us something about church life when people have to face persecution and complacency. Then the artistry may touch us in deep personal interiors or, put another way, in heart and soul.

   The following contrast between antiquarianism and fundamentalism comes from Daniel J. Harrington. Belief that the book of Revelation speaks only to the first-century readers and is now outdated is antiquarianism. Believing that Revelation as a detailed forecast of the future is fundamentalism. Trust that God will win over evil because Jesus's resurrection means that God is victorious is the middle ground between antiquarianism and fundamentalism.[3] Many trusting Christians, including myself, believe that the only future prediction that we can know with certainty is that in the end God will defeat evil. As a very young reader of the Bible, I thought that it was best to not worry about the scary and complicated verses and focus on my favorite image of Jesus as the "bright morning star" (Rev 22:16).

3. The third mistake is belief that the beast of Revelation is a particular evil person in history. Revelation was written in a particular time and place with particular problems. The Roman government had made great progress in creating a peaceful world. In fact, life was so good the emperor was worshipped. However, emperor worship was against Christian belief. Christians faced persecution. John wrote to encourage them. The beast from the Sea is a symbol for Rome and sometimes for Satan. The "false prophet" or "beast from the earth" is the local official who carried out the worship of the emperor program and persecution of Christians.

Overview of John's Emotional Nature and Situation

Not only is Revelation scary and confusing New Testament literature; the author John of Patmos is bewildering. Sometimes when a person is difficult to understand, other people might say, "I wish I knew where he

3. Harrington, "Revelation and Millennium."

or she is coming from." Considering John's situation may help you to understand him.

A Time of Trouble

John of Patmos wrote out of deep emotions and intolerable trouble. Christianity was emerging as a new religion that was distinct from Judaism and often regarded as superstition. Although emperor worship was the order of the day, Jewish people were exempted. When Christianity was no longer a Jewish sect, Christians lost protection. Persecution and executions were possibilities. Jesus's followers needed encouragement to endure persecution. The author internalized portions of the Old Testament and drew sustenance from it. He used heartfelt imagination to express his religious experiences that convinced him of God's ultimate power and triumph over evil.

An Organizing Perspective of Good Over Evil

The author's belief in the triumph of good over evil guides his writing. His perspective is that history is in God's hands and moving towards the heavenly city of God where there is judgment and justice, rest and renewal, worship and wholeness. John of Patmos believed that vindication will come for faithful people who hallow God's name. John concluded that through the death and resurrection of Jesus, victory had already been achieved, so he expected the destruction of Rome that he called Babylon in his lifetime. His timetable was wrong, but he points towards faith in future and transcendent dimensions of divine judgment. People of all times and places who are oppressed for their faith can trust in future fairness even if they or their children do not live to see the final coming of God's will being done *on earth as it is in heaven*. John expands in an imaginative way on the theme of God's will on earth that Jesus prayed in the Lord's Prayer (Matt 6:9–13).

John and Mark both cared about the color green and had an ecological interest. Mark noted that the grass was green in the story of the feeding of the five thousand (Mark 6:39). John records that the green grass was burned up at the trumpet call of the first angel (Rev. 8:7). Locusts were told not to damage any green growth (9:4) but only people who did not have the seal of God on their foreheads. Also, like Mark, who loved green and growing things and saw something of a peaceable kingdom in the wilderness, John of Revelation had an ecological bent in his conviction that God did not want to harm the natural world. Perhaps sensitivity to nature enabled him to see symbolic qualities in frogs and locusts, lions and eagles.

Church historian Rolland H. Bainton said that Martin Luther verged on saying that excessive emotional sensitivity is a mode of revelation.[4] John's sensitivity may have invited revelation. God may have spoken to John of Patmos through John's imagination. Believers can feel certain that the powerful love of God is an objective reality and still conclude that the people utilize culturally conditioned thoughts and symbols that are stored in their inner selves. Sustaining words and visual images from his time and place melded and changed through the fire of conviction.

John of Patmos used artistic creativity to challenge and console his readers. Like Paul in Romans 8, he was convinced that God is with God's people in all kinds of terrible grief and turmoil. As an artist, he could convey ideas that Paul shared but did not develop as fully. As a theologian, Paul wrote in a literary and rhetorical way. John used visual images like an artist and poet. Both start their writing with a greeting and use a letter form. Paul concludes 1 Corinthians with the prayer "Our Lord, come!" (16:22). John concludes Revelation with "Amen. Come, Lord Jesus!" (22:20). As we have seen, Paul is convinced that death will not have the last word, and by implication sorrow, the archenemy, does not have the final say either. Yet because John of Patmos is an artist, he makes what is implicit in Paul very explicit through visual and verbal imagery of God's wiping away tears. Sorrow will be definitely defeated in John's view. He put words he must have heard in his inner voice into poetry: "And I heard a loud voice from the throne saying, 'See, the home of God is among mortals. He will dwell with them; they will be his people, and God himself will be with them; he will wipe away every tear from their eyes. Death will be no more; mourning and crying and pain will be no more, for the first things have passed away.'" (Rev 21:3–4). Because John says what Paul implies, sometimes verses from Paul in 1 Corinthians and Romans, and verses from Revelation are used together in funeral services (1 Cor 15:54–55; Rom 8:31–39; and Rev 21:3–4).

Revelation and the Old Testament

John drew meaning from Old Testament passages and more fully explains or exegetes them. Yet his end product, the book of Revelation, is a new artistic creation, not his father's prayer book.

---

4. Bainton, *Here I Stand*, 283.

John's revelation came through visions and inspired poetic recasting of Old Testament themes and images, especially of Daniel 7. Ordinary language could not convey his sightings that had to be expressed in surrealistic, symbolic images. By reading the Old Testament passages and the passages in Revelation that incorporate them, we can emotionally as well as intellectually experience how John used his past to illuminate his present.

- Daniel 7:9–14 is transformed as a vision in Revelation 1:9–20.
- Ezekiel 1:5–21 and 10:20–22 form the heavenly worship of Revelation 4:1–11.
- Psalm 96:1 becomes a new song in Revelation 14:3.
- Joel 3:13 and Isaiah 63:1–3 provide divine-warrior and harvest imagery in Revelation 14:14–20.
- Trials and tribulations in Exodus are revisited in Revelation 16:12–21.
- Tears of sorrow from Isaiah 65:17 are an ongoing part of the human condition yet are wiped away in Revelation 21:1–8.

In addition to recasting themes from the Old Testament, John used symbolic images. Babylon stands for Rome. Sexual immorality equals idolatry. The beast from the sea is the Roman emperor, and the beast from the land is the Roman official who promotes worship of the emperor. Rome is symbolized as a prostitute. The woman and child may symbolize the church and the people of God and, by implication, Mary, the mother of Jesus.

John has various images for Christ. These include: Alpha and Omega (1:8; 22:13); Almighty (1:8); Son of Man (1:13); Son of God (2:18); Amen, the faithful and true witness (3:14); Lamb (5:6, 12; 13:8): Lord our God, the Almighty (19:6); Bright Morning Star (22:16).

Revelation as drama

When I was in college, my New Testament professor, in a rare moment of departure from stress on the historical situation, shifted to a literary approach and said that sometimes Revelation is seen as seven-act play that ends with the reign of Christ and the church. Likewise, my husband heard the same explanation at a Southern Baptist college where professors read the same books as my Methodist professors.

The literary approach added to the historical criticism of my college days stressed John's literary devices and did not address his mystical visions. However, the important point is that seeing a play structure honored the dramatic quality of writing and the power of images. In retrospect, I believe that the missing piece was pastoral understanding of need for vindication and ultimate happiness when God will wipe away every tear. Students who are sad or who will in a few years minister to grieving people would do well to pause and embrace images of future vindication and consolation.

The Story Line
Introduction

John identifies his subject in verse 1: "the revelation of Jesus Christ, which God gave him . . ." John identifies himself as a brother who shared in persecution and patient endurance. He reports that on the Lord's Day, probably Sunday, he was in the spirit and had a vision of the Son of Man (a stock name for Christ). The hair on the Son of Man's head was as white as snow. His feet were like burnished gold. His voice was like the sound of many waters. (The words *as* and *like* are often used in this book in describing visions of God or Christ. These words make it clear that we are dealing with metaphor and salvation history, not science and ordinary history.) The risen Christ asks John to write what he has seen. The seven stars and seven angels are symbols with multiple dimensions.

Chapters 2 and 3 contain seven letters to the churches. The messages are from Christ to John, who writes them in seven letters and gives them to angels of the seven churches. These angels function like combined postal transportation clerks, church secretaries, and very exceptional (or even angelic) church leaders—like present-day conference ministers or bishops who are charged to make sure the churches get the point. Description of the churches and the challenges they faced gives us some historical knowledge of church life. (The churches may even sound like some churches you know.) Notice that the churches have different challenges. False teachings are a problem for the churches of Ephesus, Pergamum, and Thyatira. Complacency is blight for the churches of Sardis and Laodicea. Persecution threatens Smyrna and Philadelphia. Smyrna was poor but spiritually rich, echoing the people of Matthew's beatitudes. Philadelphia people were praised for not denying God's name (3:8), which, in this context, is Christ. People who overcome the various challenges will receive different spiritual rewards. For example, a tree of life (2:7) is the reward for Ephesians who continue to resist false teachers and who conquer the tendency to abandon their first love. People of Smyrna who rise above fear of suffering will receive the crown of life (2:10). The overall message of the seven letters is to make no concession to evil. The rest of Revelation can be divided into three parts, almost like a play in three acts—a take-off on the seven-act play concept.

Part One

Part One of Revelation is chapters 4–11. The main point is that God is the ruler of the universe. Christ as the slain Lamb—the crucified Christ—also becomes the ruler. A chapter-by-chapter summary follows. As the book unfolds following the seven letters, there are seven seals, seven trumpet events, and seven bowls of wrath, and seven end-time events woven throughout the revelatory story.

In chapter 4, Christ stands knocking at the door and thus visually introduces the image of opening the sealed book. In the heavenly court, John experiences heavenly song that glorifies the risen Christ on the throne: "And the one seated there looks like jasper and carnelian, and around the throne is a rainbow that looks like an emerald" (v. 3). Four living creatures surround the throne. Heavenly worship focuses on the worthiness of Christ: "You are worthy, our Lord and God, to receive glory and honor and power, for you created all things, and by your will they existed and were created" (v. 11).

Chapter 5

The Lamb, symbol of Christ, is worthy to open the scroll with seven seals. The living creatures sing a new song: "You are worthy to take the scroll and open its seals, for you were slaughtered and by your blood you ransomed for God saints from every tribe and language and people and nations; you have made them to be a kingdom and priests serving our God and they will reign on earth" (vv. 9–10).

Chapter 6

The Lamb opens the seven seals. A white horse, and a rider with a bow that is a symbol of divine chastisement or victory, come from the first seal. A red horse, a symbol of death in battle, emerges from the second seal. The third seal releases a black house that represents famine. The fourth seal, a pale green horse, symbolized plagues and death. The fifth seal opened to show how many martyrs had died. They cried, "Sovereign Lord, holy and true, how long will it be before you judge and avenge our blood on the inhabitants of the earth?" (v. 10). The Lamb is more powerful than kings are, and in control of history. There is peace in the presence of God and the Lamb. The sixth seal reveals an apocalyptic cataclysm that will be even more intense than the scenario in Mark 13.

Chapter 7

The people of God emerge victorious, sealed out of every living tribe of the people of Israel. They are robed in white, the garments of purity, because they have been purified by the sacrifice of Christ: "For this reason they are before the throne of God, and worship him day and night within his temple, and the one who is seated on the throne will shelter them. They will hunger no more, and thirst no more; the sun will not strike them, nor any scorching heat: for the Lamb at the center of the throne will be their shepherd, and he will guide them to springs of the water of life, and God will wipe away every tear from their eyes" (vv.15–17).

Chapter 8

The angel breaks the seventh seal, and for a while there is silence. Then seven angels with seven trumpets blow them and release all kinds of trouble. Hail, fire, and blood as in Exodus 7–10 plague the earth. A mountain falls into the sea. The hope is that people will be shocked enough by this dire imagery to redirect their lives.

Chapter 9

More woes come. Despite locusts, plants and tress escape harm (9:4). Some humans who had escaped the woes did not repent from worshipping idols of bronze, stone, and wood.

Chapter 10

A mighty angel comes down from heaven with a little scroll. John asks the angel to give him the little scroll (v. 9). The angel says that the scroll will be bitter in the stomach but sweet as honey in the mouth. When John eats it, the scroll tastes sweet but makes his stomach bitter. John is called or commissioned to prophesy (v. 11). His message will be bittersweet. Suffering will be bitter, yet ultimate triumph will be sweet.

Chapter 11

After more woes there is transformation of the kingdom of the world to the kingdom of God. God's temple in heaven, a counterpart to the Temple in Jerusalem, is laid open. John paints a verbal picture of Christ the ruler. God's justice is a stake: "We give you thanks, Lord God Almighty, who are and who were, for you have taken your great power and begun to reign" (vv. 17–18). The song continues, noting the rewarding of servants, prophets and saints.

Part Two

Part Two of Revelation is chapter 12 through chapter 20. In this section, there is a horrific war with the dragon and beasts. The dragon represents Satan and the beast symbolizes Rome. God wins.

Chapter 12

Satan, the dragon, puts his anger into the beast, the Roman empire. The woman clothed in the sun, with the moon under her feet, is the people of God or the church, and by implication, Jesus's mother (v. 1). The woman may also symbolize Israel giving birth to the Messiah. Thus, the image is "polyvalent"; that is, the image has more than one meaning. Her offspring are those who keep God's commandments and maintain their testimony to Jesus. In the heavenly war, Michael and his angels fight the dragon. The woman escapes to a safe place with the help of eagle's wings (v. 14). The dragon is enraged and goes off to fight her children, who represent the church.

Chapter 13

The beast makes war. John calls for the endurance and faith of the saints (v. 10). The symbolic number for the beast is 666. (John's favorite number is seven, so six is definitely defective.) The "beast from the sea" is the emperor. The "beast from the land" is an official of Rome, who promotes worship of the emperor and of the goddess Roma.

Chapter 14

The companions of the Lamb are saved and sing a new song that only the redeemed can sing. These companions are people who have died and had the strength and integrity to refuse to worship idols. There is no rest for emperor worshipers. John reports his vision of the gathering of the righteous and the judgment of the wicked in a metaphor of harvesting grain that is based on Joel 4:13.

Chapter 15

In a preview of the end, verses 3 and 4 are the centerpiece of the book, with the theme of all nations worshipping God: "Great and amazing are your deeds, Lord God the Almighty! Just and true and your ways, King of the nations! Lord, who will not fear and glorify your name? For you alone are holy. All nations will come and worship before you, for your judgments have been revealed" (15:3–4). Their song is based on Moses's song in Exodus 15:1–18. Seven plaques are given to angels to use.

Chapter 16

Through the seven last plagues that are disasters greater then germ warfare, God gives Babylon, a symbol of Rome, a great deal of pain. These disasters include sores, blood, sunburn, and darkness that are poured from the seven bowls. The hope of the Exodus promise is fulfilled in Christ. God remains the people's redeemer and judge of the oppressed.

Chapter 17

John has a vision of the great whore as a symbol of Babylon and Rome. She sits on a beast that has ten horns and seven heads (17:5–7).

Chapter 18

Babylon falls. "'Fallen, fallen is Babylon the great! . . . and the merchants of the earth have grown rich from the power of her luxury'" (vv. 2–3). "And the merchants of the earth weep and mourn for her, since no one buys their cargo anymore" (v. 11). Economics and morals are connected, as Old Testament prophets Amos and Micah well knew. The day of Babylon's fall was not a good day for the Roman Board of Trade! The martyr's prayer for God's vengeance in Revelation 6:10 is answered in chapter 18. There is vindication: "Rejoice over her, O heaven, you saints and apostles and prophets! For God has given judgment for you against her" (18:20).

Chapter 19

There is rejoicing in heaven. God reigns, and heaven opens. The kingdom of God is stronger than Rome. There is a white horse, with Christ as the rider called "Faithful and True" (v. 11). Christ as a wise warrior is also called the Word of God. Christ is superior to rulers of the Roman Empire and is called "King of Kings" and "Lord of lords"(v. 16).

Part Three

Part Three of Revelation is chapters 20–22. The main idea is that peace and harmony are restored. God wipes away every tear. Death does not have the last word. Christ is victorious. God dwells with people. Persecuted people of any time and place can find consolation and hope in the message of triumph of good over evil.

Chapter 20

There is a first battle and then the first resurrection, where faithful people enjoy peace for a thousand years. Satan is released from prison and is in a very short time (relatively speaking) defeated forever. Those who have died are judged according to their deeds (v. 12). There is a hint of universalism here.

Chapter 21

Voices and visions promise that God will wipe away every tear and make all things new:

> See, the home of God is among mortals. He will dwell with them; they will be his peoples, and God himself will be with them; he will wipe every tear from their eyes. Death will be no more; mourning and crying and pain will be no more, for the first things have passed away. (vv. 3–4)

A vision of the New Jerusalem includes light and glory of the Lord in this heavenly city. There is no need for temple or light, which comes from the glory of God. There is no night: "I saw no temple in the city, for its temple is the Lord God the Almighty and the Lamb. And the city has no need of sun or moon to shine on it, for the glory of God is its light, and its lamp is the Lamb (vv. 22–23).

Chapter 22

The angel shows John the river of the water of life, the tree of life, and the heavenly worship. "On either side of the river is the tree of life with its twelve kinds of fruit, producing its fruit each month; and the leaves of the tree are for the healing of the nations" (v. 2). There is an invitation:

> "It is I, Jesus, who sent my angel to you with this testimony for the churches. I am the root and the descendent of David, the bright morning star." The Spirit and the bride say, "Come." And let everyone who hears say, "Come." And let everyone who is thirsty come. Let anyone who wishes take the water of life as a gift. (vv. 16–17)

The last book in the Bible ends with an invitation that flows into a benediction, which captures a deep yearning for grace. The desire for grace is in itself a blessing: "Come, Lord Jesus! The grace of the Lord Jesus be with all the saints. Amen" (vv. 20–21).

The World in Front of the Text

Reading

If reading the whole book of Revelation is overwhelming, here are some short passages that you might like to read:

1. Christ's words in John's vision of Christ (1:9–18).
2. The heavenly worship (4:1–11).
3. A song of victory and rejoicing in heaven (19:1–2).
4. A promise of presence (21:3–4).
5. Glory of God (21:22–26).
6. Jesus as the bright morning star (22:16–17).

Looking at Art

Edward Hicks painted many variations of his most famous theme, which is the peaceable kingdom. Sister Wendy brings us one of his paintings.[5] Images of the peaceable kingdom depict chapter 11 of the Old Testament book of Isaiah. Edward Hicks wanted to represent peace between people and animals that is depicted in Isaiah. In my sense of things, this painting also neatly matches the peaceful and harmonic conclusion in Revelation. In Hicks's painting, Native Americans and American settlers are at peace together. Wild animals and children rest in the shade of a tree. I recall words in Revelation that speak of the redeemed: "They will hunger no more, and thirst no more; the sun will not strike them, nor any scorching heat" (7:16).

Furthermore, it seems to me that the restoration of the heavenly city, which is like a new Garden of Eden, echoes the peaceable-kingdom theme in Isaiah 11. *Harper's Bible Commentary* states that the eschatological restoration of Eden, like conditions that are found in Isaiah, are important in apocalyptic thought.[6] In Revelation the heavenly city is Eden restored as a state of mind and sense of place.

Making an Art Project

Using polymer compound or self-hardening clay that can be found in many craft stores, create a lion and a lamb, or another combination of animals to symbolize the peaceable kingdom. Surprising friends include bear and butterfly, cat and dog, elephant and mouse, leopard and skunk, badger and bunny. Use your imagination to think of others.

---

5. Beckett, *Sister Wendy's 1000 Masterpieces*, 204.
6. *Harper's Bible Commentary*, 1318.

Bibliography

Art History and Theological Aesthetics

Apostolos-Cappadona, Diane, editor. *Art, Creativity, and the Sacred: An Anthology in Religion and Art*. New York: Crossroad, 1984.

Beckett, Wendy, and Patricia Wright. *Sister Wendy's 1000 Masterpieces*. New York: DK, 1999.

———. *The Story of Painting*. New York: Dorling Kindersley, 1994.

Canaday, John. *Keys to Art*. New York: Tudor, 1964.

Dillenberger, Jane. *Style and Content in Christian Art*. Nashville: Abingdon, 1965.

Flora, Holly, and Soo Yun Kang. *Georges Rouault's Miserere Et Guerre This Anguished World of Shadows*. New York: Museum of Biblical Art in association with D Giles Limited, London, 2006.

Janson, H. W. *History of Art: A Survey of the Major Visual Arts from the Dawn of History to the Present Day*. Englewood Cliffs, NJ: Prentice-Hall, 1962.

McCurdy, Charles, editor. *Modern Art: A Pictorial Anthology*. New York: Macmillan, 1958.

Phaidon Press. *The Art Book*. London: Phaidon, 1994.

———. *Annunciation*. London: Phaidon, 2000.

———. *Crucifixion*. London: Phaidon, 2000.

———. *Descent*. London: Phaidon, 2000.

———. *Last Supper*. London: Phaidon, 2000.

Rouault, Georges. *Miserere*. Boston: Boston Book and Art Shop, 1963.

Simon, Linda. *Genuine Reality: A Life of William James*. New York: Harcourt Brace, 1998.

Snyder, James. *Medieval Art: Painting–Sculpture–Architecture, 4th–14th Century*. New York: Abrams, 1989.

Weismann, Donald L. *The Visual Arts as Human Experience*. Englewood Cliffs, NJ: Prentice-Hall, 1974.

Bibles

Joint Committee on the New Translation of the Bible. *The New English Bible*. New York: Cambridge University Press, 1971.

Meeks, Wayne A., et al., general editor. *The HarperCollins Study Bible: New Revised Standard Version, with the Apocrypha/Deuterocanonical Books*. New York: HarperCollins, 1993.

Smith, J. M. Powis, Edgar Goodspeed, et al., translators. *The Complete Bible: An American Translation*. Chicago: University of Chicago Press, 1939.

Bibliography

Biblical Studies and Christology

Aune, David. "Revelation." In *Harper's Bible Commentary*, edited by James L. Mays, et al., 1300–1319. San Francisco: Harper and Row, 1988.

Bailey, James L., and Lyle D. Vander Broek. *Literary Forms in the New Testament: A Handbook*. Louisville: Westminster John Knox, 1992.

Bridges, Linda McKinnish. *The Church's Portraits of Jesus*. Macon, GA: Smyth and Helwys, 1997.

Brown, Elizabeth. "The Meaning of Perfection in Matthew." *The Unitarian Universalist Christian* 53 (1998) 24–29.

Brown, Raymond E. *An Introduction to New Testament Christology*. New York: Paulist 1994.

———. *An Introduction to the New Testament*. New York: Doubleday, 1997.

Caird, G. B. *The Language and Imagery of the Bible*. Philadelphia: Westminster, 1980.

Cousins, Ewert. translator. *Bonaventure*. Classics of Western Spirituality. New York: Paulist, 1978.

Crownfield, Frederic R. *A Historical Approach to the New Testament*. New York: Harper, 1960.

Duling, Dennis C., and Norman Perrin. *The New Testament: Proclamation and Parenesis, Myth and History*. Fort Worth, TX: Harcourt Brace, 1994.

Fitzgerald, John T. "Introduction to 2 Corinthians." In *HarperCollins Study Bible: New Revised Standard Version, with the Apocrypha/Deuterocanonical Books*, edited by Wayne A. Meeks et al., 2164–66. New York: HarperCollins, 1993.

Fuller, Reginald. "Matthew." In *Harper's Bible Commentary*, edited by James L. Mays et al., 951–82. San Francisco: Harper and Row, 1988.

Gomes, Peter J. *The Good Book: Reading the Bible with Mind and Heart*. New York: Morrow, 1996.

Goodspeed, Edgar J. *An Introduction to the New Testament*. Chicago: University of Chicago Press, 1937.

Haight, Roger. *Jesus: Symbol of God*. Maryknoll, NY: Orbis, 1999.

Harrington, Daniel J. *The Gospel of Matthew*. Collegeville, MN: Liturgical, 1991.

———. *How to Read the Gospels: Answers to Common Questions*. Hyde Park, NY: New City, 1996.

———. *An Invitation to the Apocrypha*. Grand Rapids, MI: Eerdmans, 1999.

———. *Paul's Prison Letters: Spiritual Commentaries on Paul's Letters to the Philippians, and the Colossians*. Hyde Park, NY: New City, 1997.

———. *Revelation: The Book of the Risen Christ*. Hyde Park, NY: New City, 1991.

———. *Romans: The Good News according to Paul*. Hyde Park, NY: New City, 1998.

———. *What Are They Saying about the Letter to the Hebrews?* Mahwah, NJ: Paulist, 2005.

———. *Who Is Jesus? Why Is He Important? An Invitation to the New Testament*. Franklin, WI: Sheed and Ward, 1999.

Hooker, Morna D. *The Gospel according to Saint Mark*. Peabody: MA: Hendrickson, 1991.

Keck, Leander E., editor. *The New Interpreter's Bible*. Vol. 8, *New Testament Articles, Matthew, Mark*. Nashville: Abingdon, 1995.

———, editor. *The New Interpreter's Bible*. Vol. 10, *Acts–First Corinthians*. Nashville: Abingdon, 2002.

———, editor. *The New Interpreter's Bible*. Vol. 11, *Second Corinthians–Philemon*. Nashville: Abingdon, 2000.

———, editor. *The New Interpreter's Bible*. Vol. 12, *Hebrews–Revelation*. Nashville: Abingdon, 1998.

Bibliography

Krentz, Edgar M. "Introduction to 1 Thessalonians." In *HaperCollins Study Bible: New Revised Standard Version, with the Apocrypha/Deuterocanonical Books*, edited by Wayne A. Meeks, et al., 2218–19. New York: HarperCollins, 1993.

Lohfink, Gerhard. *The Bible: Now I Get It! A Form Criticism Handbook*. Translated by Daniel Coogan. Garden City, NY: Doubleday, 1979.

Lohse, Eduard. *Colossians and Philemon: A Commentary on the Epistles to the Colossians and to Philemon*. Translated by William R. Poehlmann and Robert J. Karris. Edited by Helmut Koester. Hermeneia: A Critical and Historical Commentary on the Bible. Philadelphia: Fortress, 1971.

Mays, James L., general editor. *Harper's Bible Commentary*. San Francisco: Harper and Row, 1988.

Parales, Heidi Bright. *Hidden Voices: Biblical Women and Our Christian Heritage*. Macon, GA: Smyth and Helwys, 1998.

Pelikan, Jaroslav. *Jesus through the Centuries: His Place in the History of Culture*. New Haven: Yale University Press, 1985.

Rensburger, David K. "Introduction to the First Letter of John" In *HarperCollins Study Bible: New Revised Standard Version, with the Apocrypha/Deuterocanonical Books*, edited by Wayne A. Meeks, et al., 2292–93. New York: HarperCollins, 1993.

Rowell, Edmon L., Jr. *Finding God in the Rest of the Story*. Macon, GA: Smyth & Helwys, 1998.

Smith, D. Moody. "Introduction and Commentary to the Gospel of John." In *Harper's Bible Commentary*, edited by James L. Mays, et al., 1044–76. New York: Harper and Row, 1988.

Stackhouse, John G., Jr. "Wounded Healers." *Sightings* February 7, 2007. Chicago: University of Chicago Divinity School, Martin Marty Center. No pages. Accessed May 31, 2007. Online: http://martycenter.uchicago.edu/sightings/archive_2007/0222.shtml.

Tillich, Paul. *Dynamics of Faith*. New York: Harper, 1957.

www.ingramcontent.com/pod-product-compliance
Lightning Source LLC
Chambersburg PA
CBHW062036220426

43662CB00010B/1523

An Artistic Approach
to New Testament Literature